NO FEAR
ZEN

"No Fear Buddha." Charcoal drawing. Isabel Collins, age 5.

NO FEAR ZEN

Discovering Balance in an Unbalanced World

Richard Collins

Hohm Press
Chino Valley, Arizona

Cover Design: Adi Zuccarello, a.zuccarello@gmail.com

Cover Image: *Wrestling Balance*, © 2002, a bronze sculpture by James E. McKie, Jr., www.mckieart.com

Interior Design and Layout: Becky Fulker, Kubera Book Design, Prescott, Arizona.

Library of Congress Cataloging-in-Publication Data

Collins, Richard, 1952- author.
  [Works. Selections]
  No fear Zen : discovering balance in an unbalanced world / Richard Collins.
    pages cm
  Includes index.
  ISBN 978-1-935387-95-4 (trade pbk. : alk. paper)
  1. Zen Buddhism. 2. Zen Buddhism--Doctrines. I. Title.
  BQ9266.C65 2015
  294.3'927--dc23
                    2014047873

pp. 113–115: excerpts from, "The Man on the Dump" from THE COLLECTED POEMS OF WALLACE STEVENS by Wallace Stevens, copyright © 1954 by Wallace Stevens and copyright renewed 1982 by Holly Stevens. Used by permission of Alfred A. Knopf, an imprint of the Knopf Doubleday Publishing Group, a division of Penguin Random House LLC. All rights reserved.

Hohm Press
P.O. Box 4410
Chino Valley, AZ 86323
800-381-2700
http://www.hohmpress.com

This book was printed in the U.S.A. on recycled, acid-free paper using soy ink.

So as I always say: come to zazen, climb into your coffin; after zazen, climb out of the coffin. What's the difference? Nothing to fear.

—Robert Livingston Roshi

In the ups and downs of life, we're deceived by the difference in the balance.

Saying, "I've had satori!" is only feeling a difference in the balance. Saying, "I'm deluded!" is feeling another. To say food tastes delicious or terrible, to be rich or poor, all are just feelings about shifts in the balance.

—Kodo Sawaki

CONTENTS

Discovering Balance in an Unbalanced World

THESE DISCUSSIONS OF ZEN practice are the verbal record—both spoken and written—of a decade or more of reflections on my engagement with the practice of zazen and with my teacher Robert Livingston Roshi, Abbot of the New Orleans Zen Temple. It is also the record of my engagement with my own students, since I have found it is the student who certifies the teacher. Each teacher is a nexus of inheritance and legacy, a recipient of a great gift from the past and a bearer of great responsibility to the future. Most of all, even though addressed to a general audience, this book is a record of my own struggles with Zen, especially with the role of bringing a great faith in everyday Zen practice into balance with a great doubt in the meaning of existence in an unbalanced world. The assertions expressed here as pronouncements and certainties are the result of many hours of taciturnity and uncertainty. Like the Finger Sarira of the Buddha, these words are the traces of those struggles left in the ashes of a great fire of doubt, but in the end they are only words, charred finger bones pointing at the moon.

Nevertheless, because they are the result of experience, they point the way without fear of contradiction.

The title of this collection is intended to capture the spirit of Zen in the tradition of Taisen Deshimaru and Kodo Sawaki, a spirit of concentration on the great matter of life and death in the uncompromising attitude of the samurai, the spirit of "No Fear Zen." Whatever we may think of the specific actions of those Japanese warriors or the causes they fought for, we must respect the concentrated effort of discipline and self-sacrifice that marked their distinctive way of life. And in a world that requires bravery and decisive action in addition to generosity and compassion, we can learn much from the now-extinct samurai in creating a new kind of bodhisattva warrior for peace in the twenty-first century.

Part I, "Delusion Itself Is Satori," comprises two short personal narratives about my practice, both as a student and as a teacher, and a list of six things that Zen is not about. The first narrative was written for the occasion of my master's eightieth birthday in January 2013. It was read aloud at this celebration, along with other tributes from disciples, monks and bodhisattvas, some of which were sent from afar and abroad. It is a discontinuous but mostly chronological narrative of significant moments, spots of time, we might say with Wordsworth, in which the spontaneous overflow of powerful feelings (let's call them moments of satori for shorthand) are recollected and reflected upon in tranquility. The second narrative describes a visit to the prison in Tehachapi, where I was asked through Prison Dharma Network to provide instruction in Zen practice to the inmates. This short piece was published in the Bakersfield *Californian* and online at SweepingZen.com. Our group, the

Zen Fellowship of Bakersfield, continues to navigate the bureaucracy to provide regular service to these inmates. The third piece, on six misconceptions about Zen, was the basis of a talk I gave with Gary Enns to the Bakersfield Area Skeptics Society, a tough but open-minded audience whose belief in science and reason had little on the radical skepticism of Zen doubt.

Part II, "Everyday Practice of the Way," contains primarily *kusen*[1] and *mondo*, spontaneous oral teachings and dialogs delivered during and after zazen to groups of one or two to twenty practitioners during introductions to Zen practice, *sesshin* (retreats), or daily or weekly zazen with *sanghas* in New Orleans and Alexandria, Louisiana, and Bakersfield, California. Most of these were recorded or recollected immediately afterward and then edited for print. Since kusen and mondo are spontaneous events addressed to the moment and the specific situation, and to a private (or actually semi-public) audience of sitting practitioners, some context or further explanation is sometimes needed to capture the tone and thrust of the exchange.

These talks have been arranged without regard to chronology but according to four subjects of practice: Shikantaza (zazen, or just sitting), Attachment, Ceremony, and Ordination. This sequence roughly coincides with the beginning practitioner's journey from learning about posture and breathing, to asking questions about the meaning of practice in relation to basic questions of Zen and Buddhist thought, to moving from being an observer of ceremony to a

---

[1]   Foreign words not normally contained in a regular English language dictionary are italicized the first time they are used in this text. These and other words specific to Zen practice are defined in the Glossary.

participant in it, and finally (for some) the decision to take *bodhisattva* (lay) ordination.

Part III is my commentary on the swordsman and *ronin* Miyamoto Musashi's *Dokkodo*. It is dedicated to Dr. Michael Flachmann, an inspirational Shakespeare scholar and fifth dan black belt in judo. These reflections on discipline, compassion, and the way of bodhisattva strategy were composed in a state of what might be called contemplative shock in the weeks following his sudden death in 2013. There has been much soul-searching and hand-wringing about the appropriate role of samurai or Budo Zen, focused on discipline and self-sacrifice, and what might be called pacifist Zen, focused on nonviolence and compassion. This supposed dichotomy is only a matter of emphasis, however. Budo Zen may focus on the determination of the martial artist Bodhidharma while pacifist Zen focuses on the serenity of the enlightened Buddha. One arrives at compassion through concentration, the other at concentration through compassion.

The particulars of practice as described here are in the tradition of Budo Zen, the Zen of "no fear." In this tradition the importance of the emptiness (*ku*) of all phenomena (*shiki*) puts our own lives in perspective with all other phenomena, which are also empty of substance. We learn this through the practice of zazen, from which we emerge not as nihilists intent on shortening our allotted time, but as humanists dedicated to enriching the brief existence we share with all other beings. We can do this only if we are unafraid of life and death, if we are able to, as Hakuin said, "die now!"

I am indebted to the audiences of these spoken words for their attention, dedication to practice, and insightful questions and comments. This includes the members of the two groups I founded (or who found me). I would especially thank Margaret Waring, Robert Savage, and Larry White of the Zen Fellowship of Alexandria, Louisiana, as well as Gary Enns, Scott Burton, Paul Boatman, Portia Choi, Josh Shin, Patrick Blake, and Andy Kendall of the Zen Fellowship of Bakersfield, California. Thanks go, too, to my family—Leigh and Isabel and Cyleste, especially—for their indulgence in my penchant for exploring paradox and for never taking the easy way, something that has not always made it easy for them to live with or without me.

Many thanks, too, to Jeff Cantin and Greg Smith, intrepid pillars of the New Orleans Zen Temple. To Tony Bland of Mississippi, my brother monk and dharma heir of Robert Livingston, as guide and pathfinder. And to Reiryu Philippe Coupey, Robert Livingston's brother monk and close disciple of Deshimaru, I owe a longstanding literary friendship and brotherhood in Zen practice in spite of the fact that we have never met in the flesh. Above all, I am indebted to Robert Livingston Roshi for his guidance and confidence in my imperfect abilities; these words are a tribute (and tributary) to his thundering silence.

August 2014
Carpinteria, California

I

Delusion Itself Is Satori

bonno soku bodai

The true nature of delusion is Buddha-nature;
The empty body of illusion is the Dharma-body.
—Shodoka

On the Occasion of My Master's 80th Birthday

A Personal Recollection:
January 27, 2001 to January 27, 2013

1. Introduction to Zen

In my calendar for 2001, there is a notation in black ink: "Intro to Zen: 8:45 AM to 2:00 PM." The date was January 27, exactly twelve years ago today. In my journal I wrote: "Exhausted after introduction to Zen practice at the New Orleans Zen Temple. Robert Livingston, the abbot, did not disappoint. In the line of direct Zen descendants, if not just grumpy old men, he has all the bearing of a true Zen monk." Not that I knew what a true Zen monk was, of course, aside from what I had read. But from what I had read, he could hold his own with Ikkyu, Hakuin, or Daruma himself. "Gruff humor," I wrote, "along with a bit of warm condescension."

We were shown around the temple by Jason, the young monk from Texas, and Mario, the German resident, from Patrick's Bar and Restaurant on the ground floor to the kitchen and sewing room on the fourth floor. The second floor held the reception, dojo, and workrooms; on the third floor were the office, his wife Elizabeth's painting studio, and the residents' cells. Someone asked Jason why he came to New Orleans to study Zen. He said, "It was very down to earth here. Some of these places can be so New Agey. And the food at the temple is fantastic!"

Robert's first kusen was a good introduction to his spontaneous oral teachings during zazen. I'm sure he must have boomed something about posture and breathing, something about attitude of mind, about the knees pressing the ground, the buttocks pressing the *zafu*, the head pressing the sky. But what struck me, and what has stuck with me, is the core teaching about the essential question of life and death and their relation to zazen. He said: "Come to zazen, climb into your coffin. Leave zazen, climb out of your coffin. What's the difference? No fear!"

After that first zazen the ceremony had a powerful effect on me. What I had at first glance taken to be someone's red and black motorcycle helmet on a shiny round pillow turned out to be a large lacquered two-hundred-year-old *mokugyo*[1]. This first time chanting the *Heart Sutra* was moving for me. During *mondo* I wanted to ask ten thousand questions—but where would I start? Every one of them would have sounded so intellectual and so shallow and beside the point. Soto versus Rinzai? Do you ever use koans in *dokusan*? I wanted to know all the details of ceremony and dojo etiquette. I also wanted the big answers to the great questions. But I was willing to wait, to practice, to sit, and to let the answers, if there were any, show themselves.

In the *Denkoroku: Record of the Transmission of the Light*, Keizan gives each "transmission" from master to disciple a formulaic structure: there is a mondo (or interview) in which the master says or does something that results in the disciple having satori, taking the precepts, and shaving his head.

---

[1]   Foreign words not normally contained in a general English language dictionary are italicized the first time they appear in the text. These and other words specific to Zen practice are defined in the Glossary.

These almost always occur during the very first meeting between master and disciple. This is a curious compaction of a process that, like all learning processes, more accurately takes months, years, or decades. The kernel of truth, though, is that the original teaching drawn from a first impression of a teacher is what draws someone to the practice, and while this first teaching may lie dormant, like a seed planted, it is usually the root of what sprouts and blossoms later as a revelation. For me, I climbed into my coffin on that first day, and when I climbed out, I realized that what I got from Robert was: "delusion itself is satori." He didn't say this, but he embodied it with his being. I heard it again later in Kodo Sawaki's saying that "satori is like a thief entering an empty house," and later still in Deshimaru's teachings on *ku* and total abandonment.

I left the temple that day in January, twelve years ago, thinking this was just what I was looking for: discipline and practice. I could wait for whatever it was that came after that, whether it was answers to my questions or just more questions. I returned the next day, and the day after that, for the next five years, climbing in and out of my coffin. It has made all the difference.

2. Sake Cafe

In August of that year, Robert invited me to lunch one Sunday after zazen. We went to Sake Cafe on Magazine Street just after it had been transformed from a purple and white K&B drug store into a postmodern sushi bar. I left my bike in his van, which seemed to be still running as we locked it up.

We sat at the bar and drank hot sake and cold beer, and ate gyoza and squid salad with our sushi as we exchanged life stories. Robert had been married three times, and so had I. He had spent some of his youth in Los Angeles, and so had I. He had lived for many years in Europe, and so had I. He had a daughter, and so had I. He came to Zen in his forties, and so had I. There, though, the similarities ended. Twenty years older than I, Robert had made and lost a lot of money. His adventures in Europe as a recovering alcoholic, former casino owner and international fugitive seemed far more romantic than mine as a poet and scholar. He'd first come to New Orleans in 1952 at the age of nineteen, the year I was born. I arrived in Louisiana in 1982, about the time that he came back from Europe and built the temple.

When we went out to the van, we discovered that it was locked. The keys were inside, in the ignition, and yes the van was still running. It had been idling for the entire two-hour lunch. I thought I'd noticed the motor running, but surely the Zen master who took care of all existences was aware of his environment here and now and would not have left his keys in the ignition and the motor running! I must have been mistaken. Or maybe it was a teaching?

While we waited for his wife to bring the extra set of keys, we had another drink and covered some more of his life story. By the time Elizabeth got there, I was determined to help him write his memoirs someday. Had Robert not locked his keys in the van I might have persisted in seeing him as the stuff of legend, a distant superhuman Zen master; instead, the sake, the beer, the sushi, the life stories, and the forgetfulness brought him down to earth, made him human.

This was a teaching, the most valuable teaching of all. Never again would I assume that he was infallible. Never again would I assume that I was wrong when I saw him make a mistake. This would allow me to point it out to him when he was making a mistake and in this way we could help each other.

3. The Underpants Sutra

August 20, 2001. During zazen Robert talked about the upcoming *bodhisattva* ordination, for which I was planning, and the necessity for strong practice. Those who were serious about practice needed to get their own robes and zafu. "The zafus in the dojo," he said, "are for tourists, the dilettantes of Zen, for those who come one time or only once in a great while, not serious practitioners. Using another person's zafu is like wearing their misfitting, dirty underpants." Christine and Jason laughed out loud. Mario said later that he couldn't help laughing, either. I wasn't laughing; I was too busy thinking Robert was talking about me. It turns out that everyone thought he was talking about them. Josh said he was too afraid to laugh: "I just kept hoping he wasn't going to say my name!" That would have been bad indeed. Imagine being immortalized in the *Underpants Sutra*.

4. 9/11

The night of September 11, 2001, I came for zazen with Mario in the dojo. We were the only ones there. I recall the images that came to mind during zazen. Mario and I were the Bamiyan Buddhas that the Taliban had blasted out of the side of the cliff along the Silk Road in Afghanistan six months earlier. We were the Twin Towers, our ribs pierced by jets, crumbling in our own skins.

The next morning Robert came to zazen and sat with us. I wondered if he would use the occasion for a lesson in *mujo.* He chose silence, throwing us back on ourselves, on zazen. Somehow this silent teaching made the ceremony that morning more meaningful. As he did *sampai* I noticed his hair had grown out a little, just a bit of white stubble, as though he had neglected to shave his head for the last couple of days. Afterward, he said to me, "Richard, you must learn how to play the *inkin.*"

On the way home I noticed the workers on their way to their offices looking up at the tall buildings on Poydras Street. I knew what they were thinking; I was looking up there too.

5. Dreams

Deshimaru put no stock in dreams. Robert puts little stock in words. So it's interesting that Robert has sometimes taught by speaking in my dreams.

September 2001. I dreamed I kept falling asleep during zazen and couldn't wake up. On the wall in front of me appeared Robert's shadow holding the *kyosaku.* I felt the stick touch my shoulder and tried to bend left but kept weaving. The kyosaku came down gently but firmly on my right shoulder and then on my left shoulder. This dream was not unique. It showed my anxiety about not being able to "wake up," my concerns about what was lacking in my practice, and my feeling that Robert could at any moment be severe with me, as he has been with others, when actually he has never been anything but gentle and firmly encouraging even in his criticism. I am reminded of Dogen telling how he had satori when the fellow next to him got whacked with the kyosaku, and mind and body dropped off.

October 2001. I dreamed Robert called me out onto a balcony during zazen and said, *"Mu."* He looked somehow like

Muhammad Ali. I began to laugh and kissed him on the lips. He said, "Do you understand?" I said, "Yes! No!"

February 2002. I dreamed I was sitting in the dojo and I began to fall asleep. Robert said, "Richard, wake up!" and leaned over to nudge me in the ribs, but as he did so he tipped over completely, awkwardly, and couldn't get up again without my help.

6. Why a Master?

January 2003. I've been asked why I have need of a "master." I don't entirely understand it myself, but it has something to do with my inadequate answer: "I trust Robert; he is my teacher." It also has to do with him as a representative of the lineage, part of the line of direct transmission all the way back to the Buddha. Or if that's just a pretty story, all the way back to Bodhidharma. Or if that's just a myth, back to Dogen. Or if that's just a Soto dogma, back to Taisen Deshimaru and Kodo Sawaki. Or if that's just an illusion, the relationship between Robert and me is enough.

Something else, and more to the point, about the master question came clear one day during zazen. Having one master makes you master of everything else, including yourself. Unlike religious fanatics who give themselves to an invisible savior or L. Ron Hubbard, I know Robert would never ask me to do something crazy the way Jehovah asked Abraham to kill his son. He wouldn't ask me to put on a dynamite suit. I've had close friends, though, who have asked me to do things that were almost that crazy. But they are not my master.

People who think they are their own masters—like those who make up their own religion—are usually mastered by their job, their family, their friends, their ambition, their addictions, their regrets, their desires, or their illusion that they are their own master. They always have that lack, that desire, the very lack and desire that dissipate during zazen and through Zen practice. Devoting yourself to your master, you need never bow to anyone or anything ever again. But of course you *do* bow—to all existences—because there is no fear. No fear of being mastered and so no fear of mastery. A fearless man is not a masterless man. A fearless man knows his master, and since master and disciple are one, the disciple is master of himself when the master recognizes him, and the master is the disciple of the disciple just as the disciple is master of the master.

7. Another Dream

March 2003. My wife Leigh dreamed we were at Robert's house for lunch. We were in the kitchen and Robert was saying how I needed to work through the difficult things and not quit. For example, just because I accidentally hit him on the neck with the kyosaku, I shouldn't be afraid to lead. I needed, he said, to "get right back on that kyosaku and ride!" With that he mounted the kyosaku like a wooden pony and galloped around the kitchen. I told this dream to Robert and he laughed for a long time.

8. Genmai and Guinness

Once, on one of Robert's birthdays, after zazen at *genmai* we substituted Beck's beer for tea in the teapot. When the server tipped the teapot to fill Robert's bowl to wash out the grains of rice, a golden foam billowed in his bowl. Unimpressed, he said, "What's this?" and then "Where's the Guinness?"

9. Great Palace

Taikaku, Robert's monastic name, I'm told, means Great Palace. The temple has always reflected Robert's hope for a robust Zen practice in New Orleans. Ample space was dedicated to all the functions of the practice, from zazen to various kinds of *samu*. There was living space for the residents, a sewing room to make zafus and *rakusus*, an art studio space for Elizabeth to paint in, a rooftop garden for his plants, a commercial grade kitchen for creating worthy *tenzos*, and rental space on the ground floor to provide revenue to make the temple self-supporting. This is Muhozan Kozenji, No Peak No Shore Temple, and it is the Great Palace Robert has created for the *Dharma*.

10. After Katrina

Robert threw a party on July 4th, 2005, just weeks before Katrina. After that, I did not see Robert again for five years. Katrina forced us, Leigh and our three-year-old daughter Isabel and me, to evacuate to Central Louisiana and then to California. Later we moved to Alexandria, where we had first landed in our evacuation route. I was asked to establish a sitting group there, which became the Zen Fellowship of Alexandria. Sometime in 2009 three of my students there expressed interest in ordination. So one morning I returned to the temple in New Orleans and sat in my old beginner's seat. At *kinhin* I went out to get a drink of water. Robert embraced me with a smile and said: "I thought that was you. I recognized you by your posture." It was as though I had never left. After genmai we had a couple of St. Pauli Girls in Robert's quarters and caught up on the last five years. He agreed to ordain my students from Alexandria and weeks later, as we made plans for the ordination *sesshin* over the phone, said in passing: "You have worked hard for a long time. You should take monastic ordination."

11. How's the Weather?
If my bodhisattva ordination was a shattering experience that changed my worldview, monastic ordination was no big deal. I was more interested in my students' ordination during the same ceremony. A few years later, though, Robert gave me permission to teach, which is conferred in the *shusso* ceremony during sesshin. Like bodhisattva ordination, becoming shusso was another worldview changing experience, mostly because this time it was not about me. During the ceremony the new shusso makes an admission of inadequacy. This admission was for me not just a formality; it was a sincere expression of my humility in the face of the great responsibility of teaching Zen.

Next came an exchange between master and disciple that at first struck me as absurd and superficial. I approached Docho Roshi (as he is called in the ceremony) and performed my three prostrations. To my astonishment, I rose up to meet the eyes not of Docho Roshi (the ceremonial actor) but of Robert (my human teacher, the very one who had left his keys in the van at Sake Cafe, the one who in Leigh's dream rode the kyosaku around the room like a wooden horse, the one who delivered the *Underpants Sutra*). I recited the lines I'd memorized from the script, grinning: "Recently the weather has been pleasant, Docho Roshi. How is your life?" Robert grinned back: "Well," he cracked wise. "I'm alive!"

It was much needed comic relief and perfect for the ceremony. I had not known in rehearsal it would come out like this; all the preparation had not prepared me for the moment of understanding when master meets disciple on this human level, acknowledging the years they have spent in each other's company getting acquainted with their abilities, failings, and gifts. So at this high moment of great tension, tension can be dropped. It is the master saying, "Don't worry. You have practiced a long time. You have worked hard. There is no turning back now, no matter how badly you fuck up. We are all of us only human. Today is a good day. Let's enjoy it."

What looks like a silly "have-a-nice-day" exchange has an important function essential to the ritual's emotional logic, its dramatic wisdom. The exchange about the weather is a public acknowledgement of the bond between the master and the new shusso. It brings the formality and solemnity of the occasion down to a personal and human level, nothing special. Traditionally, this moment is followed by sharing tea and cakes, but we dispensed with that and had a few beers after the sesshin instead.

12. Celebrating Here and Now

Today we drink again to celebrating not only Robert's eightieth birthday but also thirty years of Robert's teaching in the temple. My story with Robert spans only a dozen years and is just one of many stories in the three decades which have seen the ordination of ten monks, scores of bodhisattvas, dozens of residents, and hundreds of tourists—"the dilettantes of Zen," as Robert called them—who attended introductions or perched for a time on borrowed zafus. Each of them has a story, each one a part of the temple's history and Robert's legacy.

In ten years we can look forward to Robert's ninetieth birthday celebration and then his hundredth. I suspect he will outlast many of us here. I am sure that what will outlast all of us is the influence of the New Orleans Zen Temple, which is indeed what its name describes: Muhozan Kozenji—a Mountain with no Peak, a River with no Shore.

For now, though, we honor Robert's teaching and this temple by celebrating *here and now*.

Sitting Behind Bars
in Tehachapi

Nothing is separate, nothing is missing. Everything is present.
Why go elsewhere when you can practice the Way here and now?
—Dogen, *Fukanzazengi*

I VISITED THE PRISON in Tehachapi as a guest chaplain for some inmates who requested a Buddhist priest to conduct services for them. As the director of the Zen Fellowship of Bakersfield, I was contacted through the Prison Dharma Network, a group that coordinates visits to prisoners throughout the U.S. It took several months of paperwork and delay, but at last I was entering the first of many gates.

About forty miles from Bakersfield lies the dry, stark, windblown Cummings Valley of the Tehachapi mountains, high enough for scrub oak but too low for evergreens. Among a scattering of houses and vineyards sprawl the cement and steel compounds of the eighty-year-old California Correctional Institute, the third oldest prison in California after Folsom (1880) and San Quentin (1852).

The prison opened in 1933 as the California Institution for Women, Tehachapi, the first women's prison in the state, with twenty-eight inmates transferred from San Quentin where they had been housed side-by-side with men with predictable results. The new women's prison was run on progressive lines with the idea that these women (those who were not hanged) could be returned to society better than they came in. They were allowed to make "colorful frocks" fashioned after what was chic in the magazines and were even encouraged to wear red shoes if they liked, rather than the drab prison garb and dull boots they had sported in San Quentin.

It was into that environment that Humphrey Bogart as Sam Spade sent Mary Astor as Brigid O'Shaunessy at the end of *The Maltese Falcon* (1941): "Well, if you get a good break, you'll be out of Tehachapi in twenty years and you can come back to me then. I hope they don't hang you, precious, by that sweet neck." James M. Cain also referenced the prison in *Double Indemnity* (1943) as the destination for a wife who had been cleaning her gun when her husband "got in the way."

There was a reason Tehachapi became a byword in the noir films of the 1930s and '40s. First, the progressive prison was a new concept and in the news. Also, crimes committed by women like Burmah White (L.A.'s own version of Bonnie Parker) were on the rise with the breakdown of traditional family values that came with the economic hard times of the Depression and the Dust Bowl migration to California (most of the several hundred female inmates in Tehachapi during its "boom" years in the '30s were, unlike Brigid O'Shaunessy, from the Los Angeles area). You can read more about its history in Kathleen A. Cairns' *Hard Times at Tehachapi: California's First Women's Prison* (2011). The prison closed after the 1952 Tehachapi earthquake that also destroyed much of downtown Bakersfield and reopened as a men's prison two years later.

When the airport-like metal detector went off in spite of my having taken off my shoes and emptied my pockets, the guard asked me what that was around my neck, indicating my rakusu, the bib-like garment given to me by my master when I was ordained. I rarely wear my rakusu outside the dojo where we practice, but I did today. Along with my driver's license, it's all I'm allowed to carry inside. "It's a religious thing," I said. "Oh," said the friendly guard, passing his wand under my arms and between my legs. "I thought maybe it was some kind of bag. You're good to go."

Research has confirmed the value of various kinds of meditation in prisons, even for the most hardened criminals (and jaded guards). Although many wardens and chaplains have shown some resistance, resistance has softened with the hard data that shows a decrease in recidivism for prisoners with an established meditation practice. And substantial anecdotal evidence suggests that prisoners who meditate become model prisoners while still incarcerated. One study estimates the economic benefits of meditation in prisons resulting in annual savings of more than $31 million, with about half of the total benefitting correctional institutions and half society at large (David L. Magilla, "Cost Savings from Teaching the Transcendental Meditation Program in Prisons," *Journal of Offender Rehabilitation* 36:1-4, 2003, 319-331). Most studies have focused on TM, Vipassana, and mindfulness meditation techniques, but for rehabilitation purposes the differences between techniques appear to be negligible.

One program in Alabama that focuses on Vipassana is the subject of a documentary called *Dhamma Brothers http://www.dhammabrothers.com.* Testimony from the prisoners is extraordinary and moving. "For the first time, I could observe my pain and grief," states inmate Omar Rahman. "I felt a tear fall. Then something broke, and I couldn't stop sobbing.

I found myself in a terrain where I had always wanted to be, but never had a map. I found myself in the inner landscape, and now I had some direction." Another inmate tells how his practice helps him navigate prison life: "When someone cuts in front of you in the chow line, the first reaction is to push him. The Vipassana technique gives you a mental tool to observe the situation. If you give yourself time to think, you are gonna come up with a better solution."

The idea is simple: meditation opens a window on the self and its relation to the rest of the world that causes each person to take responsibility for the consequences of his or her actions.

My sponsor and guide is Deborah, a decade-long veteran of prison ministry. We drive past D Block, a relatively peaceful place, where she says they keep former gang members, sex offenders, and homosexuals for their own safety. Occasionally they add a lifer to the mix. Lifers tend to have a calming effect, she said, because they don't like others disturbing the peace of what they consider their home.

Our destination is C Block, where the general population of convicts resides. The fifteen-foot fences are topped with gleaming spirals of razor wire like great ominous Slinky toys. As we approach each inner gate, it opens ahead of us and shuts behind us, seemingly on its own, as though the gates themselves sense our coming and going. I am reminded of the third of the bodhisattva vows: *hommon muryo seigan gaku*—"Dharma gates, however many they may be, I vow to pass through them all."

The chapel is a nondescript, dingy room with a dirty linoleum floor on a hallway with classrooms on either side. Eight inmates file into the room, and we shake hands and introduce ourselves. They range in age from twenties to fifties, black, Hispanic, white. A couple of them already have an established personal practice. Some are curious. All want to improve their lives.

We push aside the bright orange plastic chairs and spread the grey woolen blankets that serve as cushions. They show me the meditation postures they use on their bunks in their cells. I invite them to try sitting my style for a while, focusing on those new to the practice. One fellow who has been assiduously taking notes is slouching. He seems accommodating, aiming to please. His posture expresses a kind of submissiveness that I have seen cured in the past by a few months of diligent zazen. I come up behind him and press my fist into his lower back, straightening his spine. I get him to lift his collarbone, tuck in his chin, and gaze straight ahead.

"Look at him," I say. "Look at his posture. How intimidating he is. He looks like a goddamn samurai."

I turn down the hard fluorescent lights and the room immediately feels more congenial, more human. In the semi-darkness we let our minds quiet in the silence, pay attention to our breath, and let our hopes and regrets drop off. This is zazen, just sitting, being here and now. Here and now might not sound like much when you're confined to prison, but when you realize that it's all there really is, it's not so bad. What is painful is obsessing about how things should be, how things might have been, if only....

I compare this clarifying process to the settling of a muddied stream. You can't clarify the water by continuing to stir it up. As Kodo Sawaki said, "Zazen is good for nothing." You have to do nothing; then clarity can arise, even here in the belly of concrete and steel bars. Afterwards we discuss the first half or so of Dogen's thirteenth-century instructions on doing zazen, the *Fukanzazengi*, which says, "Nothing is separate, nothing is missing. Everything is present. Why go elsewhere when you can practice the Way here and now?" Our time is up for today. We shake hands again all around. They thank me, and I thank them. These inmates are hungry for more, more books, more DVDs, more mala beads, more help with their practice. They especially want more access to teachers. I would like to encourage other teachers to join the Prison Dharma Network and to offer their services to inmates who request it. The work is satisfying and needs doing.

The IBS (International Buddhist Sangha) in San Diego has in the past come to Tehachapi, but it's a long trek from San Diego. The Buddhist scholar Lewis Lancaster discusses his years of work with IBS in California prisons in an interview [*http://www.youtube.com/watch?v=A6_IFFXbM14*] in which he mentions collecting about ten thousand books for the prisoners in California, about a thousand of which were given to Tehachapi. Although they have been approved by the censors, these books had yet to reach the shelves or the inmates when I was there.

I look forward to going back. In the meantime, the inmates can sit on their own, like monks in a do-it-yourself monastery, knowing that they are not forgotten or alone.

Six Things Zen Is Not About

Our own sneeze is the entire universe.
—Kodo Sawaki

THERE ARE A LOT of preconceptions about Zen and Buddhism. And since there are so many sects and lineages, and so many offshoot groups inspired by but not adhering to Buddhist practice, perhaps anything one says can be true of some "meditation" group somewhere. This is especially true now, when there are so many freelance, self-appointed "teachers" who have little to do with any lineage but have instead created their own hybrids of various practices, from pop psychology to tantra and yoga, with the well-intentioned goal of suiting Eastern wisdom traditions to current Western sensibilities.

It is remarkable how many teachers (both bona fide lineage holders and freelancers) came to practice as professional therapists, and this has given much of American Buddhism in the last thirty or forty years its decidedly therapeutic bent, offering "insight" or "mindfulness" or any number of other worthy but elusive mental health benefits. As in any free marketplace of religious ideas, a certain amount of this jockeying for position in the American self-help market might be healthy in the long run, if for no other reason than that it breeds a healthy skepticism of self-appointed gurus and cure-alls. The Buddhist ancestry of many of these practices has lent them a certain legitimacy and in more than one case the core strength of their success. But hybrids in plants are like alloys in metals: they can either fortify the final product or dilute it so much that it becomes fruitless or worthless. Too often, hybrid meditation practices have good intentions but no coherent structure or discipline to sustain them once the feel-good feeling turns less than good—or less than a profit. In the Soto Zen lineage that comes down from Dogen Zenji in the thirteenth century to Kodo Sawaki and Taisen Deshimaru in the twentieth, to my teacher Robert Livingston and his disciples' groups in the twenty-first, we focus on the practice of zazen (seated concentration) and samu (work practice) above other aspects such as scholarship, koan practice, mindfulness, and so forth. We believe that how one breathes is more important than what one believes and that one's posture is more important than what one professes. That seems clear enough. Still, it might be a good idea to clear the ground of some preconceptions about Zen practice and to state in clear terms what, in our view, Zen is *not* about.

1. "It's not about you." You sometimes hear students speak of "my" zazen or "my" practice, as though Zen practice is something that concerns only them, or even worse that it is something they have some ownership of and control over, as though it is up to them alone. This phrase "my practice" is insidious because it assumes that it is about you yourself alone. The more one practices, the more one realizes that "you" are just the beginning.

The bodhisattva ideal presumes a few concepts that have deep significance for every branch of philosophy from how we perceive things (aesthetics) to how we know things (epistemology) to how we treat others (ethics) to how we exist (ontology). Two notions basic to Buddhism are impermanence (mujo) and dependent origination, or the interrelatedness of all things. These give rise to a third notion, more difficult to comprehend for us in the West, of *anatta* (*anatman*, or *muga*: no-self). We could talk all night about the fine points of the "no-self" idea, but basically it does *not* mean that you don't exist, only that "you" don't exist. What do I mean by that? Just this: that it's not that there is no self but only that there is no substantial, transcendental, metaphysical self that pre-dates or postdates your physical incarnation here and now. If there is no substantial self, then maybe there is no self to claim this practice as "mine."

Let me qualify this statement a bit: we can certainly say this is "my" practice if we are talking about the superficial benefits of stress reduction and relaxation—the yoga of Zen, if you like—which are both superficial and minimal. Stress might actually increase for some: it depends on what they find in their concentrated state and how they react to what they find. After all, zazen is only a mirror, but it is a mirror like a vampire's mirror: nothing is to be seen there, no self. Because zazen is not about you, most people, assuming that it is about them and finding out that it's not, will take off after a quick introduction or a few sittings. The others, those who stay and stick with the practice, find that they are not getting themselves up in the morning and dragging themselves to the dojo in the dark for themselves but for their family, or for their extended family, or for their colleagues, or ultimately for all existences. This is when "my" practice becomes "the" practice. What you find is that the self keeps changing; the practice provides the thread of continuity in that constantly emptying construct called the "myself." As Kodo Sawaki said, "Precisely that self which I haven't thought up is who I really am." So it is not that the self doesn't exist, it's that you can't ultimately know what that self is. And that's not a liability, it's the foundation of great liberty.

2. "It's not about cultural beliefs." Because Zen practice is not about you it cannot be about beliefs in specific ideas. Ideas, like other phenomena, including Buddhism itself, are mutable, impermanent, although also interrelated. Three notions that are actually cultural and are often associated with Buddhism but that have nothing to do with true Zen practice—at least in their popular or traditional senses—are: karma, reincarnation, and vegetarianism.

Karma and reincarnation, at least as these are usually thought of, as rewards and punishments for ethical or unethical behavior, are inconsistent with the notion of no-self. In terms of punishment, what would be spanked? In terms of reward, what would be reborn on a higher plane? Even the Dalai Lama has questioned the traditional notion of reincarnation. But if karma is simply action and its causes and effects, any action has origins and consequences. What if reincarnation is simply a mythological way of expressing the recirculation of energy and matter, simple physics rather than metaphysics, or rather physics mistaken for metaphysics?

The question is: does science assert, as Buddhism does, that change is the only constant in the universe and that all existences are interrelated? Are these notions compatible with scientific notions of biology, chemistry, and physics? I think so. Scientism, or faith in science, is the cultural belief of contemporary America (fringe religionists notwithstanding); scientism is the belief that frames how we explain what we can't explain. When my daughter was nine and considered herself a scientist, she said she did not believe in God because she believed in science. I said, "Even some scientists believe in God." She said, "Dad, I said I believe in *science*, not scientists." That's a nice distinction, but it also shows that there are many ways to believe, many ways to express faith—in science, in experience, or even in skepticism.

3. "It's not about becoming a better person." Many people come to Zen practice as a method of self-improvement. My own master found Zen as part of his Twelve-Step program. But Zen practice is not about becoming a better person. Such a notion might bring you to Zen, but if you persist in thinking that it is a method of self-improvement, you won't last long. It follows, of course, that it could not be about becoming a better person because it is not about you. Maybe you want to be a vegetarian or a vegan because you think it makes you a better person—maybe you think it improves your karma, even if only your karmic digestion, or because you believe that ethically you should not eat meat, either because you don't want to harm living creatures, or because it is better for your health, or because you think it is better for the environment. In each case it is because you perceive the interrelatedness of all existences. Fine, but don't get a big head about it and think you're a better person because of this. Your arguments about it being better for the environment and all living beings might hold water, but the moment you wave these arguments like a flag of righteousness you've lost the argument because it has become all about you.

In the same way, sitting concentration may or may not improve your mood and thus make you less of a pain in the ass to those around you. If so, that's a good thing. But let's not get carried away and say that you are in some way a better person for this, just as a well-fed and well-trained tiger is a better tiger to have in the house, but it doesn't change the fact that the tiger has teeth and claws and instincts that can still be sharp once the food runs out or the trainer turns his back. The Buddhist precepts exist in many forms as lists created to keep the potential dangers we pose to ourselves and others in check, hundreds for women, dozens for monks, a handful for everyone else, and one that encompasses all the rest for our lineage: zazen. Why only one? Because "following the precepts" is shorthand for what is likely to occur if you practice zazen. That is, you will naturally tend to do less of the things that harm others and yourself.

The *sila* (or ethical) dimension of Buddhism is to be found in taking the precepts. But the highest precept of all is practicing zazen. This is because zazen leads us back to the precepts naturally, automatically, unconsciously, spontaneously. Similar benefits ensue thanks to any regular discipline and attention to the details of taking care of one's surroundings, including the body. Benefits no doubt ensue from zazen but you cannot pursue them directly. If you have the slightest sense of a goal, a great chasm opens up and widens; you have created a dualism and you have lost the battle. Consider the student who is always interested in the grade versus the student who is always interested in doing the work at hand—which one will succeed? Zen is not about doing what you need to do to become a better person; Zen is doing what needs to be done.

4. "It's not about spirituality." In the dojo where we practice, we have a long flat stick of hardwood on the altar: it is called the kyosaku, the "wake-up stick." It is used to strike those who request it during zazen when they are feeling sleepy or agitated in body or mind. It comes down on the shoulders—*whap! whap!*—and sends your tension down through your body into the ground. Its effect on those around you is also bracing and salutary. On our kyosaku is written in calligraphy: "No spiritual significance." Whenever I hear the word spirituality, I reach for my kyosaku. Manjusri, the bodhisattva of wisdom, carries a sword to cut delusion. The wooden kyosaku is our practice sword. The kyosaku cuts through the delusion of spirituality.

5. "It's not about enlightenment." What is this enlightenment everybody talks about as being the "point" of Zen? Is it awakening to some purer reality than the one we are in? I don't think so. Is it second cousin to the Enlightenment of eighteenth-century scientism, empiricism, encyclopedism, and rationality? Not at all. What is the common conception of it, then? Not even Buddhists can agree on this. What we know is that it is not a culminating state. It is not something from which there is no return. Indeed, it is no different than the natural state. It is a return to the natural state. If satori awakens us, then it must wake us up to delusion as much as to truth, the truth of delusion and the delusion of truth. What is satori? Delusion itself is satori. Delusion itself is enlightenment.

In his commentary on the *Shodoka*, Kodo Sawaki quotes that poem's most important lines: "The true nature of delusion is Buddha-nature. / The empty body of illusion is the Dharma-body." When it comes to enlightenment, we know one thing for sure, says Kodo Sawaki: "'I am enlightened'— these are the words of an intolerable boor."

But to know this we need to be aware of our delusion. How can we be aware of our delusion? Practice zazen. In Dogen's time there was a doctrine of "original enlightenment," but it made Dogen ask the question: "If I am already enlightened, why do I need to practice?" He went all the way to China to find out. And when he came back, when asked what he discovered, he answered: "Nose over navel; ears over shoulders." Because, simply put, practice is enlightenment. This sounds like something that needs to be taken on faith, but actually it means just the opposite: it has to be taken as more than an idea, more than an attitude. It has to be earned through experience. It can't be pilfered through intellectual means from others who have done the work of practice. Kodo Sawaki said, "Satori is like a thief entering an empty house. There is nothing for him to steal."

6. "It's not about ideas." Most of all, Zen is not about ideas. That's why it can't be found in books. You can read all you want about it. You can talk about it with others, but you are just talking "around" it. You can even "understand" it and know all about Zen, its history, its luminaries, its literature, its ideas, but you can't know Zen from the outside, intellectually. This is why I invariably avoid interfaith discussions of Zen. Well intentioned as they are, they always seem like a good idea, but in looking for common ground everyone misses the point, which is the uncommon ground.

Certainly Zen is fascinating, its personalities seductive, its literature fabulous, its art endlessly inspirational—and it happens to have the most voluminous literature of any Buddhist branch and the most prolific and wide-ranging art—but Zen is not its literature or its art. Zen is not its philosophy. It is not its thought. There are lots of clever people who know "about" Zen, who can allude to the koans and stories in an essay or a joke, but you can tell someone who has not practiced Zen a mile away because it's not about ideas, it's not about enlightenment, it's not about spirituality, it's not about becoming a better person, it's not about cultural beliefs, and it's not about you.

II

Everyday Practice
of the Way

*All the Buddhist scriptures are
only a footnote to zazen.*
— Kodo Sawaki

On Shikantaza

Let's Not Talk about Zen

Words can't be escaped so they might as well be useful.

TO SAY "LET'S NOT TALK about Zen" in a book about Zen might seem paradoxical but it's not really. Zen is a word that gets tossed around a lot without a very clear understanding of what it means. I used to get a Google alert every time Zen was mentioned in a blog or news item on the Internet. Most of it was nonsense. Zen most often appeared as a product name, nightclub, restaurant, or spa to evoke an aura of serenity or cool. When I taught a seminar on Zen Literature at Xavier University in New Orleans, I asked my students on the first day to ask ten people what they thought Zen was, and they came up with some interesting responses, including "a brand of tea," "a massage parlor," and "a gay cult." No one said that it was a sect of Buddhism that originated in China under the influence of Taoism as a "direct pointing at the mind," and a "mind-to-mind transmission of wisdom" from master to student, "a direct pointing at the mind," "not dependent on words," and "without benefit of scripture." No textbook definitions, in other words.

This "without scripture" reference is sometimes interpreted as without words. But why then are there so many stories, koans, poems, and sutras in the Zen tradition? Why so many witty and wise verbal exchanges attributed to Zen masters? What does it mean to say that when we talk about Zen it's only a way of pointing at the moon?

Ultimately, this tension between direct experience and words is a tension between being and believing, between practicing and professing, between being present and representation. For someone like me, a creative writer and literary scholar by training and tendency, the paradox of a practice that doesn't place a high value on the benefit of words required a leap of faith, a "great abandonment" of everything I had gathered from my education. My master must have recognized this when he gave me my monastic name, Taisen or Great Abandonment.

Zen teachings have had a long history of ambivalence with the word. The spoken word has been the preferred medium of communicating what can (and cannot) be conveyed in words, whether through mondo (question and answer dialogues, often very brief), *teisho* (Dharma talks or lectures), and *kusen* (spontaneous oral teachings during zazen peculiar to the lineage of Kodo Sawaki and Taisen Deshimaru). Writings have traditionally favored those forms that fit well with the oral tradition, such as poetry and essays. Zen is a practice, not a belief, so how one sits is more interesting than what one says. How one breathes is more important than what one believes. Still, we can begin by talking about why we don't talk (much) about Zen.

If this sounds paradoxical, welcome to the world of Zen. Language is suited to expressing dualistic concepts—yes/no, right/wrong, either/or—but language, which is based on difference, takes some massaging to express non-dualistic concepts. The great philosopher-monk Dogen Zenji is not an easy read. His prose is reminiscent of James Joyce or Gertrude Stein, Lewis Carroll or Martin Heidegger. It is often incomprehensible to the rational mind. To say, for example, that to forget the self is to study the self (and vice versa), one must hold two opposite ideas in mind at the same time before you can go on to the rest of the ideas expressed in his "Being-Time," such as that the self encompasses myriad existences. Or when one of the Zen poets says, "I don't bow to Buddhas," we have two competing claims implied: reverence embodied in irreverence, irreverence embedded in reverence. Welcome to the language of Zen.

One way to talk about Zen without paradox would be to describe it without editorial or philosophical commentary. "Here is what we do in Zen: We enter the dojo, we bow, we sit, we get up, we bow, we walk, we bow, we sit, we eat, etc." Actions not ideas. Verbs not nouns. Not very interesting, you might say, not very enlightening, not very Zen, as we might have been led to think of it. I've had people come to Zen sesshin, extended sitting retreats of a half-day to several days, and be very disappointed that there was not more going on, or at least something different going on, something that would fit the Google alerts image of Zen. As one fellow who didn't last past breakfast said, "I thought you guys were supposed to be laid back. But you eat fast and then start working. You don't even enjoy your food. This is hard!" I said, "We enjoy our food; we just enjoy it very efficiently. We don't need to talk about it."

I was asked by the Unitarian Universalist Fellowship of Kern County, California to give a "sermon." I prefer to call it a talk. A sermon sounds so grand, something much grander than what I have to offer, something that should be delivered from a mountaintop or at least on a mount. I looked up a few definitions for *sermon*: "1. A religious talk: a talk on a religious or moral subject given by a member of the clergy as part of a religious service, or: 2. A long lecture on behavior: a long and tedious talk, especially one telling somebody how or how not to behave." While I am an ordained monk and therefore a "member of the clergy," I suppose, I am not qualified to pontificate on religious or moral subjects, much less to lecture anyone—tediously or otherwise—on right behavior. In my tradition, the Japanese Soto Zen lineage of Kodo Sawaki and Taisen Deshimaru, we don't get sermons as such.

We do get kusen, spontaneous oral teachings given by the *godo*, or teacher, during zazen. Kusen are not meant to be grasped by the critical, discriminating mind (we have enough of that kind of activity in our everyday life). The non-discriminating nature of kusen is embodied in the way it is delivered and received. The person in zazen sits facing a wall, silently, concentrating on breathing and posture, allowing the words of the godo to wash over them, neither accepting nor rejecting their claims. The kusen is the verbal equivalent of the mental state of zazen. The kusen makes no argument. Some kusen are as short as "Concentrate!" Others are longer than the Gettysburg Address.

So, zazen is Zen, and zazen is sitting. It is not talking. Zen is practice.

But what is Zen practice? Zen practice is very simple. It is sitting in a quiet place for a set period of time, every day, silently, paying attention to posture and breathing. It might also include other practices that accomplish the same purpose through action: archery, flower arrangement, martial arts, sports, the arts, theatre, poetry, gardening, or your own work as teacher, dishwasher, mechanic. It is living non-dualistically and non-judgmentally here and now.

Zen is the practice of sitting and letting body and mind drop off. It is the art of sitting and forgetting. Bringing us back to the here and now, Zen connects us with what can't be paraphrased in well-put ideas. Zen takes us beyond reason and logic, beyond faith and the irrational, into the heart of reality. Zen disperses our preconceptions. Zen reminds us to be humble in the face of death and the unknown. Zen centers us and, just as importantly, de-centers us. It forbids us to speak and it requires us to speak. It won't allow us to worm our way out of the difficulties of life but forces us to face them directly with courage and dignity, without fear.

"When we come to zazen we climb into our coffins; after zazen, we climb out of our coffins. What's the difference? No fear." This is not an alternate state but our original, natural, spontaneous state of mind. The great Rinzai monk Hakuin said, "Young people, if you fear death, die now!" He was not recommending suicide but rather exhorting us to face the abyss of the emptiness of zazen, to recognize our existential dilemma, and to give up our attachments to the world so that we can embrace the richness of the world more fully and without fear.

Very simple. Very difficult. Not easy, not difficult.

Words can't be escaped so they might as well be useful. In our lineage there are a few essential terms. Let's cover just three here: *mushotoku, hishiryo,* and *mujo.*

Mushotoku: no profit, no personal gain, no object, no split between self and other, subject and object, you and me. Thus no attachment.

Hishiryo: thinking not-thinking; not "non" thinking and not "thinking thinking" but thinking not-thinking.

Mujo: constant change, mutability. This is the nature of all things, self and other, due to their having no substantial identity, being empty.

The *Heart Sutra* manages to cover all three of these notions through a fourth: the interchangeableness of *shiki* (phenomena) and *ku* (emptiness, *sunyata*), or what might be called phenomena-emptiness. More commonly, this is translated as: "form becomes emptiness; emptiness becomes form."

These three essential terms do not include many of those we might normally associate with Zen Buddhism, such as *Enlightenment, Awakening, Mindfulness, Nirvana, Karma, Satori,* and so on. In fact, we rarely use any of these words in our Zen practice because they are just not very useful. Some lineages do make much of these terms, but in ours the practice of mushotoku mind in the practice of zazen is so basic, so powerful, and so suggestive, that it is enough to fortify a lifetime of practice.

Every morning, after zazen, we chant the *Hannya Shingyo*, or *Heart Sutra*. We do not chant it in English but in a mixture of ancient Sanskrit, Chinese, and Japanese. Why not in English? It's simple: so that we are not tempted to intellectualize what we are chanting. Chanting is a form of music, a form of song, yes, but it is primarily a breathing exercise, a form of emptiness-practice. It is not prayer, if by that we mean any of the usual definitions of prayer. It is not: a) a spoken or unspoken address to God, a deity, or a saint; b) the act or practice of making such spoken or unspoken addresses; or c) something wished for. Chanting the *Heart Sutra* does not fit these definitions of prayer because, first, Buddhism is a non-theistic religion and so my chanting is not my personal address to any god, buddha or bodhisattva but the ritual repetition of a report of a conversation between two bodhisattvas in the manner of a Platonic dialogue. We listen and make our own conclusions but only afterwards in our study, not while chanting, because most of us don't understand the language of the chant. Second, prayer is a kind of petition, and I always hear Jim Morrison screaming "You *cannot* petition the Lord with prayer!" My desires are the very thing that cause suffering, and only through mushotoku attitude during sitting and chanting (i.e., Zen practice), do we come to hishiryo consciousness and thereby allow body and mind to drop off.

There are many translations of the *Heart Sutra*. You can find dozens on the web at *www.thezensite.org* and elsewhere. Over time Zen has adapted to its surroundings on continent after continent and each translation has adapted to the needs of a specific time and place. Its continuity is held in place less by the texts than by the direct mind-to-mind transmission of individual teachers to individual students who are part of the cross-cultural hybridization of the practice. Some will call this process a dilution of the practice, while others will call it a strengthening. Some (purists and traditionalists) will say that texts like the *Heart Sutra* lose their purity and accuracy as they travel further from their source. Others will say that as the texts get further from their source they shed the inessential cultural trappings and linguistic snares and reestablish themselves in the certainty of unmediated experience. We can shed certain cultural trappings of Indian, Chinese, and Japanese Buddhism, casting off any literal belief in deified bodhisattvas, karma as divine retribution, or reincarnation as some literal kind of metempsychosis. These are superstitions not worth preserving. But one can believe in the *Heart Sutra* not because it makes rational sense or because we have an accurate translation but because it fits our direct experience of Zen practice. In this way the continuity of the *Heart Sutra* over time and through space depends less on the textual purity or accuracy of translation than on the unbroken practice of zazen. As Kodo Sawaki said, "All the Buddhist sutras are a footnote to zazen."

Trying to Calm the Mind

*...is like trying to pick up your check
before you've done your work.*

POSTURE—SPINE STRAIGHT, hips slightly tilted forward, chin tucked in, collarbone up, shoulders under your ears. If you feel a little strain in your back, thighs, legs, just keep pulling your back straight up. Stretch the backbone, head presses the sky.

Breathing—let your lungs fill up, concentrating from the hara; let your diaphragm do the work; push down with long, slow, deep exhalations. Not very much effort to do that. Don't force it. As you practice the breathing, it will become longer, slower, deeper.

Attitude of Mind—let your thoughts pass. Don't run after your thoughts; don't chase them away; don't pursue them. Just bring your concentration back to the breathing, back to the posture. These thoughts are not really here, not really now.

We can learn everything about Zen practice through the posture and breathing of zazen. It is a dignified posture, not submissive, not pious, not proud. Strong, powerful, yet supple. The spine is straight, like the column that holds up this roof. Everything else hangs off the spinal column; all organs, muscles, limbs are relaxed. Spinal column is straight, strong.

One big mistake people make when beginning Zen practice is trying to calm the mind. This is like trying to pick up your paycheck before you've done your work. Calming the mind is a result, not a technique. You can't do it directly, only indirectly. As long as you concentrate on breathing and posture alone, the mind will calm down on its own, automatically, naturally. As long as you're stretching the backbone—letting it extend all the way from the bottom of the spine, from the lower lumbar region, up through all the vertebrae, like a string of beads or a Slinky hanging from the sky, through the neck to the head—the mind will take care of itself. So, stretch a little more, climb a little higher, pressing head to the sky. To do this, though, you need to have your back muscles relaxed. Inner organs and limbs, relaxed. Arms, legs, thighs, relaxed. Then your spine will feel supple, as though it's swaying in no breeze.

Your breath needs to be expelled in long, slow, deep exhalations. The intake of breath naturally fills up the lungs, letting the diaphragm expand, falling down, filling up the lungs, letting the belly fill. As you exhale, press up slowly, naturally, not forcing it, very calmly, until your lungs are almost empty. Then, allow those bellows to fill back up completely. This allows you to make use of much more oxygen than you use normally. This allows you to relax, to calm the mind: this is concentration.

Just try not to lust after the result. Try not to check yourself, saying, "Oh, am I calm now? Is my mind serene?" As soon as you do that, you're not calm, your mind is not serene. Just do the work of bringing your mind back to the posture and breathing. That's enough. Then you won't even need to pick up the paycheck; the benefits will be deposited directly, added to your balance automatically, naturally.

It's Up to You

Zen is a do-it-yourself operation.

WE ALWAYS SAY THAT Zen practice is not easy, not difficult, but it takes commitment, determination. Even if you can commit to only a few minutes a day, that might be enough for now. Better to sit for ten minutes every day than to skip sitting for thirty minutes or an hour several times a week. But if you sit at home and you decide to sit for ten minutes, be sure to sit for ten minutes; don't quit after five—that's worse than not sitting at all.

The difference between practicing here in the dojo and at home by yourself is that coming to the dojo represents a commitment. Here you have the support of others, you have the structure of the dojo. You're not going to be expected to do the laundry here, wash your hair, trim your nails, whatever else you have put off or need to do. All you need to do here is sit.

It's a great luxury to be able to spend time sitting. Most people are uncomfortable sitting by themselves for more than a minute or two without fixing themselves a cup of coffee, turning on the music, checking their phone, making plans, reflecting, regretting past actions. After the first five, ten, fifteen minutes in zazen, most of your stray thoughts will have come up. You might glance at the clock and think, "Ah, only five minutes have passed; it seems like ages!" And then, all of sudden, it's over. Just like life.

The point of practice is to make the most of the time we have, to realize how little time we have. The time we have to sit is not much, just a few minutes a day, or an hour—out of all the things we do, it's not much. But it can be very important. It might seem like you're not accomplishing much when you're sitting, but this can be the most productive time of the day, shedding stray thoughts, distilling energy, breathing, cutting your karma, transforming your life.

Still, not very many people come back after their first introduction to practice, very few. One in a hundred return, and even fewer develop a practice. Most people are just curious, not committed. That's fine. Even if you never sit again, having sat for just this short time can change your life. One day, you might remember what it was like. You have it inscribed in the body of your experience, in the experience of your body.

When we practice we don't practice with any expectations. When I give an introduction to Zen practice, I don't have any expectation that anyone will return, even though it would be good for me, good for you, good for each other. But even having sat for a few minutes today might transform your life. Not now maybe, but later you might think about it.

You can forget everything I said today. But remember what your body is doing right now, what your mind is doing right now. Zen is a do-it-yourself operation. Having a dojo in the neighborhood gives you structure, it doesn't give you commitment. A dojo gives you opportunity, it doesn't give you determination.

It's up to you.

Zazen Does Zazen

There is no such thing as my zazen or your zazen.

SOMEONE ASKED ME THE other day if I minded it when only a few people come to zazen. How could I be disappointed? Disappointment is the result of expectation, and zazen is done without expectation. When no one comes, a part of me is relieved. Not as in, "Oh, I'm glad no one came." What I mean is: I am relieved of my duties to oversee their zazen and free to concentrate on my own. I may sit longer. But otherwise, I sit in zazen as I always do, come rain or shine or other people. In the end there is no such thing as my zazen or your zazen, good zazen or bad zazen, alone zazen or group zazen. There is only zazen. We don't do zazen. Zazen does zazen.

Nothing Doing

In zazen, we stand still like the hummingbird.

PEOPLE OFTEN WONDER: WHAT are we doing in
zazen? Because it seems that we're doing nothing. And that
is exactly what we're doing. The rest of the day is for doing
something. A lot of something. So this is a time when we can
calm the mind by doing nothing. You can't calm the mind
by trying to calm it. You have to let it happen. So when you
do nothing, be sure you really do nothing. We concentrate
on posture and breathing; we don't think about posture and
breathing. Some teachers say we "observe" our posture and
breathing; we don't interfere with it or praise or criticize it,
we just do it and, okay, we observe it. We don't try to perfect
it. We just do our posture and breathing with our body, our
body-mind, as it is now with all its imperfections.

The effect is profound. The short-term effect is meeting
the rest of the day with energy and equanimity. The long-term
effect is wisdom that comes from discipline, wisdom that
comes from the reintegration of body and mind so that there
is no separation, so we can act spontaneously, authentically,
unconsciously, naturally.

Think of zazen as a preparation for doing things by doing
nothing, a way of distilling our energy, storing it up, cutting
our connections, our attachments, when we can stop running
after our thoughts, stop grasping at things, stop regretting
things, and just exist here and now. Just for a short time, just
an hour or so out of the day. Not much. But inertia tells us,

encourages us, spurs us to keep going, to keep doing without rest. This isn't wise. It stresses us out. It makes us sick, tired, ready to give up, unable to concentrate. Zazen is a very simple technique, very difficult to practice. Even though zazen is a form of yoga, one yogic posture sustained without any variation, yoga makes you feel like you're doing something, so maybe yoga is not so daunting, not such a challenge to our everyday frame of mind. Yoga and zazen are two sides of the same coin. Yoga is stillness in movement; zazen is movement in stillness. Yoga is very popular, its benefits appeal to the Western mind. Our Western sensibility values results, immediate results, visible benefits, measurable profits. Yet the outcomes of zazen are not always immediate or visible or measurable. Still, zazen is very important, very effective. In zazen, we stand still like the hummingbird, breathing nectar. This is all we need to do.

Shikantaza?—Impossible!

An icicle forming in the flame.

SHIKANTAZA, THIS IS WHAT we practice. It means just sitting, "only just sitting." When we come to zazen this is our whole effort. No mantras, no koans, no visualizations. No help, no crutches, no toys. This is why we call it the steep path. Very simple. Very difficult.

This doesn't mean, though, that we don't use whatever is useful. Just as we use a zafu or a chair or a bench, we can also use a koan, a visualization, a mantra. We just don't want to let these accessories turn into necessities, ends in themselves. Nothing is excluded in this practice, in this lineage. This is why we are not strict vegetarians, not tee-totalers—always the middle path. But shikantaza is all that is needed.

Shikantaza is like the four bodhisattva vows—impossible! The first vow says, "I vow to save all beings." It depends on what you mean by "I," and it depends on what you mean by "save." But most of all, it depends on what you mean by "all." I'm supposed to save all beings? Impossible! The second vow says, "I vow to drop off all delusions"—impossible! Not only impossible, not even desirable. Dogen said, "Delusion is enlightenment. Delusion is satori." The third vow says, "I vow to enter all Dharma gates"—which means I vow to enter into all forms of reality, to learn all the teachings. Good luck with that! Impossible! The fourth vow says, "I vow to follow all the way through in the Buddha Way"—yet there is no end to the Buddha Way. How can we follow through on this or any of these impossible vows?

The point is, when we sit in zazen we follow the Buddha, we get all the teachings, we drop all the delusions, we save all beings. Naturally, unconsciously.

Poetic images are crutches. But until we can walk on our own, we should use them. They can help us to grasp what we're doing. Dogen created an image: "an icicle forming in the flame." This is exactly what it's like to sit in zazen: an icicle forming in the flame. Impossible! Yet perfect. Dogen didn't say this about zazen, not directly; he said that reality is an icicle forming in the fire. One word for reality is "dharma." Dharma can mean the teachings, but the teachings are not just what is passed down orally, not what is passed down in writing, not even what is passed down in "mind-to-mind transmission." What is the teaching? The teaching is zazen itself.

When we sit in zazen, we enter most fully into the Dharma, most fully into reality, into the Way. We never enter perfectly into reality because it is not an icicle standing complete in the flame, not an icicle fully formed in the flame, but an icicle ever forming in the flame, constantly becoming, constantly working within the flame, constantly working with the flame. The spine constantly stretches up even as it melts like an icicle within our flame of flesh, this dying flame of flesh we inhabit, yet reaches equilibrium there, when body and mind drop off. All the images, all the poetic descriptions drop off, and we're left with our own experience, which all the poetic images have led us to, having helped us to understand.

So when we sit in shikantaza, only just sitting, it doesn't exclude anything. On the contrary, by not choosing anything, we exclude nothing; we include everything. Contradiction is no longer contradiction, and paradox is no longer paradox.

How Long? How Often?

True practitioners don't stick out like a shaved head.

PEOPLE OFTEN WONDER HOW often to sit, how long to sit. Is ten minutes enough, thirty minutes, forty minutes? Is once a week enough, four times a week, every day?

This innocent question has another more sinister question hiding behind it, so we have to ask, "Enough for what?" If pressed, people will answer, "Enough to get it right, to get the right effect, the benefits, the payoff." Just like when students ask, "How many pages does the paper have to be? How many quotations must it have?" They're not really interested in the length of the paper or the number of quotations; they want to know how long it has to be to get an A, or at least not to fail.

It depends. It depends not only on what you want but what you can do. It depends on the life you have, the body you have, the time you have. You don't want to throw your life out of whack, sitting too often. You have a job, a family, responsibilities, bad knees: don't neglect them to sit on your zafu all the time. On the other hand, don't neglect them by not sitting on your zafu at all.

What's too often or too long? If you're practicing with mushotoku mind, the mind of no profit, no personal gain, it should be easy enough to settle into some sort of routine, the middle path. If you're trying to achieve something, if you want "enlightenment" right away, you'll try too hard, burn out, burn your family out. It's important to take it easy, try to develop naturally. You might be ready for once-a-day sitting—that's good. You might be ready for once-a-week sitting—that's good, too. It's up to you.

I remember once at the New Orleans Zen Temple there was a debate about whether we should have shorter sittings for beginners so they could work up to the regular thirty-minute sittings, just as the rest of us used the thirty-minute sittings to work up to the forty-minute sittings of a sesshin. Someone at the San Francisco Zen Center asked Shunryu Suzuki whether it would be possible to sit for thirty minutes, instead of forty, because they had so much work to do. Suzuki said, "That's interesting because I've been thinking we should start sitting fifty minutes. So, let's compromise: how about if we sit for forty minutes?"

The point is: it doesn't matter. Once you've chosen a length of time to sit, or a day of the week to sit, stick with it. If you want to sit Wednesday evening, great, sit Wednesday evening. If you're going to sit Monday and Friday mornings, great. But don't wake up in the morning on Monday and Friday and decide whether you're going to get up and come to the dojo. Just do it. Or don't. It's up to you.

It's the same if you decide to sit for, let's say, ten minutes at home. Don't sit five, don't sit fifteen; sit ten. Later, if you want to sit longer, that's fine. Here we sit thirty minutes. Pretty light. During sesshin, we sit forty minutes. That's pretty light too. It's not the length of time you sit but the quality of sitting—and more than that, the fact of sitting.

There's a monk who runs a farm in Japan where they sit every morning for thirty minutes, then they get to work. Farming is their practice and zazen is the preparation, the reminder, the center. They have the rest of the day to farm, to concentrate, to let that morning half-hour resonate throughout the day.

I don't mind if people come to zazen for the first sitting and leave halfway through at kinhin. That's why we check the door between sittings so that someone can come just for the second sitting because that's fine too. Everyone is different. Every day is different. You do what you can. Not trying hard enough is a problem a lot of us have. The real danger, though, is trying too hard. Trying too hard can result in the "stink of Zen," when people wear their practice on their sleeve. True practitioners don't stick out like a shaved head. A bodhisattva blends in, like a ghost, not noticeable, harmonizing with the surroundings. Practice comes easily because it is not a decision, it is a given.

There's a story of a student of the sword who comes to the sword master and says, "Teach me what you know." The master says, "All right." "How long will it take if I try really hard?" asks the student. The master answers, "Ten years." "Well, then, what if I try twice as hard?" The master replies: "Twenty years!" The student is puzzled, scratches his head, asks, "Well, then, what if I give up everything else and devote myself heart and soul to your teaching, twenty-four hours a day? How long will it take?" "In that case," says the master, "you'll never learn."

A Bus Named Desire

Zazen is not an escape from the world.

WE HEAR A LOT of sounds here in Algiers Point during zazen. This morning, so far, we've heard cars, buses, and garbage trucks on the street. We've heard the train across the river chugging along the edge of the French Quarter and the Faubourg Marigny. We've heard the ferry taking passengers back and forth across the Mississippi, ships going up and down the river with cargo. Everyone going somewhere, getting something done, pursuing some goal.

At kinhin I opened the transom windows so that we could hear the sounds more clearly. These sounds remind us of the nature of our practice. Our practice in the Deshimaru lineage is a lay practice. Even as monks we are not seeking monastic separation from the busy world. On the contrary, the bodhisattva ideal demands that we sit here in the midst of the turmoil, not remove ourselves from it. Zazen is not an escape from the world, not an escape from the business of the world; zazen serves as the still point of the busy world, and we're a part of it, in the midst of it, undisturbed by it.

When I first started sitting years ago, even before I started going to the temple, I lived on Dauphine Street in the Marigny. I would sit up on the second floor of our hundred-and-fifty-year-old Creole cottage, and I would hear the Desire bus go by outside the house every twenty minutes or so. This used to be the Desire streetcar line, but now we had a bus named Desire. As I sat, I would pack up my thoughts, like a bunch of squealing monkeys, and get them ready for school. Then, as the bus came by, I'd mentally pack them inside and off they'd go for the day.

The noises we hear outside are not what disturb us; they are only a reflection of our minds. Like the surface of water, these reflections are easily perturbed, distorted. But if we can sit in the midst of these sounds, in the midst of the world, with our minds like the glass of a mirror, unperturbed in their reflection, then we might claim to be truly serene, our minds truly calm and not just a reflection of silence, not just a sponge for serene surroundings. It's easy to be tranquil on a mountaintop. What's hard is being tranquil in the midst of a Mardi Gras parade.

When we enter the dojo, we take off our shoes and leave the dust of the world outside. We can also load the garbage of our minds into the trucks outside; let them take it away. You can pack up your thoughts squealing for your attention about what you have to do today and let the bus carry them away. Let the ships take the cargo of your mind downriver and out to the Gulf. Right here and now, all we have to do is sit. Just sit.

Later, when we leave the dojo we can throw ourselves back into the midst of the action of the world, fight our battles, swim upstream, approach our menial tasks with equanimity, our demanding tasks calmly, and our disturbing issues bravely—treating trivial things as if they were serious and serious things as trivial. In this way, without discrimination, we show our respect for all things, all existences, giving them their proper weight, their proper measure, their proper due.

The Origin of This Pain Is Not in Your Back

We should not slump like bags of meat and blood.

IF YOU FEEL PAIN in your lower back or shoulders, chances are the origin of this pain is not located in your back. It might originate very far from your lower back, in your neck, your arms, your elbows, your thumbs, your mind.

It might help your posture to visualize your pelvis as a hinge—not a hinge that goes forward and backward, but one that goes in all directions, like the socket in the mount of a ceiling fan. Gravity pulls the fan, hanging from the socket, down. So your head should be: "hanging," but upward, pulling your spine away from the floor.

Sometimes during zazen we emphasize concentrating on the hara—perhaps too much. This might make the hara seem substantial, as though it is some tangible thing. It's not. The hara is empty; right in the socket of your hips and pelvis, a few inches below your navel, it's a bellows that expands and contracts, fills with energy and empties. But it is always empty, even when it's full of *ki* (energy) or fire, just as a socket or a furnace is empty, even when it is full of the ball or fire that fills it. An empty socket, the hara is the center of our concentration, but it is not something, it is not some thing.

When we sit down, making sure that our knees are pressing the floor and that our butt is solidly perched on the zafu, we should be sure to plant our spine squarely in the center of our three-point, pyramidal base, our body almost a kind of tetrahedron. As we bend in preparation for our sitting, we sway in every direction to get our bearings, to shed our "tendencies" in one direction or another—forward or backward, left or right.

When we've found that center, we don't "settle" into it—on the contrary, we continue to strive upward, stretching the spine, head pressing the sky. Instead of the vertebrae stacking one on top of the other, each weighing the others down, these vertebrae are separating, stretching upward. Sometimes you can hear them crack as they separate. Zazen is not a form of relaxation; it is strenuous concentration. The effect of zazen is tonic, energizing, vitalizing. We don't "settle into" zazen, although zazen might settle into us. We should not slump like bags of meat and blood. We have a structure as surely as a crystal vase. In zazen, we are a clear vessel into which the energy of all existence is pouring.

When we get up, we have to be careful after so much sitting not to lurch into action. As you place your thumbs in your fists and your fists on your knees, bend over each knee— right, left; right, left—two or three times. Stretch the back muscles, or rather, let them extend, don't force them. Let the muscles extend a little further with each bend, never asking more of the muscles than they can comfortably give. As you bend downward, let the air from your lungs go out and let your head gravitate toward your knee. As you rise, don't use your back muscles only, but let your arms push you up slightly. Letting your arms and your back muscles work together, you don't put too much strain on either of them, allowing your back muscles to build up their strength gradually.

Giving our attention to each of these gestures, we dispel the pain—whatever its origin—naturally, automatically, unconsciously.

Deceptively Simple

If you're bored with zazen, you're bored with life.

DECEPTIVELY SIMPLE, ZEN PRACTICE. People so easily become bored with it. Mothers everywhere have said to their children who are bored: "You have to rely on your inner resources!" If you're bored with zazen, you're bored with life. Or as Samuel Johnson said to some childish someone, "If you're tired of London, you're tired of life." If you're tired of zazen, you're tired of life.

I can understand the impulse to be always doing something. We always want life to be better. We want to build things, create, learn from the past, plan for the future, leave something as our legacy for our children perhaps. We want to arrange our lives so that we have not so many worries, not so many troubles. This takes effort. Often, in the process, we create more troubles for ourselves, more worries. There is certainly a place for doing things, making things better, acting in the outside world, the physical world, the economic world, the legal world, the political world, the social world. If we are really engaged, as we should be, with life in these appearances, we can't help but act and act and act.

But we can't be comfortable with what we do in the world if we don't have a solid sense of reality, if we are floundering in concepts of what reality is, if we take these appearances as the whole of reality. This is what zazen gives us: a sense of that real place out of which we act authentically, spontaneously, naturally. In zazen we touch those inner resources our mothers told us about, our inner London that Samuel Johnson was talking about—where we're not just distracted by the pleasures and curiosities; we're interested, invested, deeply a part of everything, of everyone, of life. This is Zen practice, impossible to be bored with, deceptively simple.

Just Mind and Body Sitting Together

…as though we are sitting for a hundred years.

SHIKANTAZA: ONLY JUST SITTING. This is what we practice. Very simple—not so easy. Many people, when they come to Zen, expect to find satori, enlightenment, or even relaxation. This is why most people—when they get their first taste of what Zen is really about, which is just sitting—find it difficult to keep their interest. They don't want to sit still; they want to be enlightened, or so they think; what they really want is to be entertained. Well, certainly the mind can be very entertaining, and so can the body. So in certain forms of meditation in which there is stillness within movement, like Tai Chi and yoga, the stillness within movement allows for this tendency to want to be distracted and entertained. That's good, that's fine. These are very good practices. But zazen, the practice of movement within stillness, is more difficult for many people. This is why shikantaza is called the steep path: no *kata* or *vinyasa*, as in the martial arts or yoga; no mantras; no koans, no paradoxes to break your head against; "no toys," as Master Uchiyama put it. Just mind and body sitting together.

Zazen is an essential practice, so basic that it predates the Buddha. Buddhist priests and practitioners would like to own it, but no one can own zazen. Nobody can claim that copyright. Before the Buddha put his stamp on zazen, it was called "the art of sitting and forgetting." Sitting and forgetting doesn't mean that we forget our past or that we go into a trance and forget the present. When we're sitting, we forget our preconceptions about reality; we let go of what we think it means to sit here, about what it means to breathe; we throw down all the complications that we brought into the room, casting off our expectations. We concentrate on the task at hand. Here and now. Not so easy—not difficult. It just takes practice.

When we sit in this posture, we sit with our spine stretching, our hips slightly tilted forward with a slight curve in the lower lumbar region so that we can get the greatest stretch. We are strong and straight, knees pressing the earth, head pressing the sky, spinal column holding up the heavens, just like the cypress column in the middle of this room that holds up the ceiling. This column has been sitting here for about a hundred years. Still, it's not really exerting much effort to hold up the building because its structure is just right. This is how we should sit—effortlessly but with structure—as though we are sitting for a hundred years.

Eventually the column in the center of the room will fall down, and we will too. If it's not taken care of, it will fall down a little faster. But eventually, no matter how well we take care of things, everything falls apart, buildings and bodies alike. We call this mujo, constant change. We live in constant dread of everything being turned upside down, in constant dread of death. So when we come to zazen we say, "Climb into your coffin." And when we leave zazen, "Climb out of your coffin." What's the difference? No fear. This is shikantaza, just mind and body sitting together for a little while, while they still can.

Like a Stake in the Ground

There is nothing inherently spiritual in this posture.

BEGINNING ZEN PRACTICE IS a matter of finding times when you can sit and then sitting. How we sit is important only because proper posture allows us to sit for a longer period of time and to return to sitting again without being anxious about the discomfort involved. Even if we sit for five minutes, though, we should sit as though we are sitting for a hundred years with no sense of beginning and no sense of an ending.

When Zen came to China, or rather when Buddhism came to China, Zen became Zen and Buddhism came to earth. This groundedness is embodied in the posture of zazen. Not that the posture wasn't there before it became the Chinese way of sitting, the posture was virtually the same all the way back to the Buddha and before. The best and most concise guide on how to sit is Dogen's *Fukanzazengi*, not written until the thirteenth century. It talks about how the spine should be raised on a cushion, buttocks higher than the legs, shoulders under ears, nose over navel, legs crossed, hands in the form of the *mudra* as though you're holding a large goose-egg just in front of your lower abdomen. Shoulders and arms relaxed, head pressing the sky—pressing the sky, not heaven. There is nothing inherently spiritual in this posture; it's just practical. Eyes kept open, cast down at a forty-five degree angle, not wide, closed enough to keep out the glare of the light, but open enough so that you don't fall asleep.

There are two temptations in zazen: one is for the mind to race in dispersion and confusion (*sanran*), the other is for it to fall asleep, sinking into darkness (*kontin*). In this as in so many other ways we want to practice the middle path. We're not trying to reach some transcendent state of consciousness. True transcendence is for us to be completely here and now. That's the difficult thing. This is why we don't have any object for our contemplation, no object for our mediation, except for sitting itself. This grounds us in the here and now, like driving a stake into the ground.

The other part of sitting is breathing. Breathing is what lightens it all up, stretches it all out. Yin and yang. Posture gives you structure without rigidity; breathing gives you volume without solidity. Gradually you feel your breath filling the cavity of your body. Allow the breath to come all the way down toward the zafu, pressing down on the inner organs, allowing the balloon to fill up, become light. Then the long, slow, deep exhalation, very slow—ten, fifteen, twenty seconds per exhalation. When you breathe in be sure you're not hunching up your shoulders—relax. When you breathe out make sure your shoulders are still relaxed, head pressing the sky. Press upward not where you had those soft spots on your head when you were a baby, the anterior and posterior fontanelles, but just between those, the crown of your head. Your chin is tucked in, your collarbone is up, eyes cast down, your neck stretching, continuing the column of the spine. The posture shouldn't change when you're breathing, the same posture, the same structure should persist. It doesn't matter whether you're sitting in *seiza*, or cross-legged in lotus or half-lotus, or in a chair. Shoulders back, eyes cast down, head pressing the sky.

Posture is relatively easy; breathing is a little harder. What's difficult is posture and breathing at the same time, effortlessly, so that your body and your mind are not distracted, just here now. Our body distracts our mind, our mind distracts our mind, so they're uncoordinated. Zazen is the simplest way to coordinate body and mind. In zazen we think with the body, act with the brain, spontaneously, automatically, naturally.

Posture and Breathing: Just Don't Choose

So we can say one's faith is only as strong as one's doubt.

ZAZEN MEANS SITTING ZEN. Sitting concentration. What we're concentrating on is just two things: posture and breathing. Don't concern yourself with your mind.

Posture is what you're sitting in now in zazen. But the particular posture doesn't matter so much—there are a lot of ways you can sit—you can sit standing up; you can sit lying down. What's important is that you concentrate on the posture. When you are sitting zazen it's important that your spine is straight, with a slight curve in the lower lumbar region at the base of the spine, so that you can sit for a longer period of time, with a good solid base, knees on the ground, your butt raised by a cushion, zafu, or chair. This puts everything in the proper alignment, so that you can allow your arms, shoulders, organs, to hang off the spine. You must have a certain amount of structure, tension without being tense, tension like the tension in a high-wire or piano wire, a natural tension, not the excess tension that is due to stress. We don't want to turn into jelly, so we constantly stretch the backbone, separating the vertebrae, allowing the energy to course up through the spine through all the regions of the body. The more you pay attention to the various channels of energy going through the body, the more you see that your body is like a diagram of an atom, with electrons orbiting the nucleus. You don't need to think about this, just become aware of it. This is the difference between meditation which has some object and Zen concentration. Concentration like orange juice concentrate, our mind compact and embodied here and now into a powerful core without the usual extraneous distractions, not watered down. Concentration as power. Power as a form of relaxation, a letting go, a gathering.

The effects of zazen are subtle. You don't realize them at first after one or two sittings, but then in daily life you find yourself relaxing in the most stressful situations and wondering why. With correct breathing you allow energy to gather more completely and more efficiently. We all know we get energy from food and drink in the form of calories. We also get energy from oxygen. Even if we take care of how we eat, we don't always take good care of how we breathe. During zazen we want to concentrate as much on breathing as we do on posture, breathing through the nose, in through the nostrils and out through the nostrils. We want to breathe all the way down into the hara, the lower abdomen. We allow the belly to flop out over the hands, let our belly expand, and when we exhale, we exhale with a long, slow, deep exhalation through the nostrils, pressing down on that bulb of the lower abdomen with the other organs, as though we're going to the toilet, pressing down, down, down. Then we allow our lungs to fill up again, fairly quickly, just a couple of seconds for the intake of breath, and then again the long, slow, deep exhalation. When our lungs are almost empty, we allow them to fill up again.

My wife is a yoga teacher, so I know that there are many kinds of breathing that can be vocalized, altered, emphasized, and so on. In zazen, though, the breath should be silent— both in the inhalation of just a few seconds, and in the long, slow, deep exhalation, which should not become an audible sigh. The length, slowness, and silence of the exhalation is crucial if it is to be extended to ten, fifteen, or twenty seconds. Filling the lungs to capacity, extending the breath down into the hara and fully into the back, should be natural and not forced, and so should the emptying of the exhalation. As you're breathing, you might notice your posture losing a bit of its structure. Let the head press the sky again. Eventually, the breathing and the posture, the pressing up of the spine and the exhalation of the breathing will work together, so that it's not really two objects of concentration, it's not posture and breathing, it's something more like posture-breathing. This is what Zen is: just one, not-two. Basically it's the same word as yoga, which means union.

Between the two periods of zazen we have kinhin, or walking zazen. In kinhin we take small steps, bearing our weight primarily on the ball of the forward foot for the length of the exhalation before taking another step while breathing in. Kinhin is a good time to concentrate on the breath, because you have a physical marker for each breath. As you step forward with each inhalation, press down on the forward foot with each exhalation. Just behind the ball of the foot is a pressure point called the "burbling spring," a fountain through which you can draw the energy of the earth by concentrated pressure. In zazen it's not quite so easy to keep our concentration on the breath as it is in kinhin. This is why in some dojos, you are asked to count the breaths during zazen. We don't count breaths, but we do follow them through observation, concentration.

The third aspect of our practice, after posture and breathing, is attitude of mind. But if you're concentrating on posture and breathing, attitude of mind takes care of itself.

The other day, after I had quoted a couple of perfectly good answers from Zen masters, Dolores asked me again, "What is Zen?" She put me on the spot. So I said I didn't know—which is true. But if we say we don't know, that's only half the story, because if you say that you don't know, that means that you know you don't know. Seung Sahn used to say, whenever his students would answer one of his questions with "I don't know," he'd say, "Just be sure that you don't know don't know."

It's very difficult to get to that one thing. Whenever we say "yes," we know there is a "no" on the flip side. In Zen literature there are a lot of paradoxes in which yes-no are spoken simultaneously. Attitude of mind, for example, is described by Dogen as "thinking not-thinking." It's not that you're not thinking, that would just be vacancy; it's not that you're thinking because that would just be cerebral stuff going on. Thinking not-thinking.

One of the hardest concepts for my literature students to grasp, especially when we're discussing late Victorian literature, is the idea that doubt and faith are not two. Faith without doubt is no faith at all, and doubt without faith isn't doubt. But when someone has a very great doubt, if they are really able to doubt strongly, logically, passionately, it takes a great faith to meet that doubt, to balance that doubt, to co-exist with that doubt. So we can say one's faith is only as strong as one's doubt. Such faith does not dispel the doubt; rather it buoys it up.

This is what we mean in Zen when we talk about "not-two." It goes back to the oldest poem in Zen literature, the *Shinjinmei*—"Faith in Mind" or "Trust in Mind"—which starts out: "Just don't choose. Don't love or hate. Don't judge. Don't discriminate. Just don't choose." Posture and breathing. Just don't choose.

We Are Not Stones

...even though we might be mistaken for mountains in zazen.

THOUGHTS ARISING DURING ZAZEN is natural. We are not stones. Just don't get involved in your thoughts. Don't push them away; don't pursue them. Let them arise and fall away. Your mind, like zazen, is like the sky. Clouds will form, naturally. You pass judgment on them only from your individual perspective, whether they are a burden or a boon. If you are a farmer, you might want clouds for your crops; if your business is solar energy, you might not care for them. If you're traveling, clouds might cause delays. If you're a tornado chaser, clouds are your bread and butter. It depends. From a certain altitude, though, you drop all judgment about clouds because they are not a problem, not a source of profit. Then you can appreciate their shapeliness, their "phenomenonity."

Zen practice allows you to develop another perspective about these thoughts. You can re-perspectivize, re-relativize them. This is really one thing that all religious practice aspires to do in sometimes very different ways: to drop your individual perspective, your preferences about whether there are clouds or not, and what type of clouds they are. You rise above them, not to become a saint, but to become acquainted with the higher altitude where clouds exist but without any notion of their being good or bad from your individual perspective. You give yourself some distance on the situation, man's situation, the tragedy and the comedy of our puny lives. This is the perspective that art sometimes gives us, out of time, eternal, the perspective that some would say is God's.

Holidays like New Year's Eve give us an opportunity to see that they, too, are nothing special. Like thoughts or clouds, holidays remind us to take them for granted, like any other day, so that every day becomes New Year's Day. Our thoughts about them put us in the center, making us think about how the past year has affected us, how we want the coming year to affect us. But when we drop all that, we rise above the days, weeks, months, years, centuries, clouds, and thoughts, so that we can see that none of them is special. We are not stones, even though we might be mistaken for mountains in zazen; our minds are unobstructed like the sky. Thoughts, like clouds, will naturally pass through our minds, but their shadows pass over our posture without the slightest effect. This is zazen: recalling that our thoughts are nothing special.

Concentration Not Meditation

Sometimes we do zazen with our bodies,
sometimes with our minds.

CONCENTRATION. WE USE THIS word often to describe what we do during zazen and in contrast to what is loosely termed meditation. Concentration does not mean thinking very hard about something. It is not Rodin's sculpture *The Thinker*. That posture, you will notice, is very different than the posture of zazen. Compare the posture of Rodin's *Thinker* to that of Kodo Sawaki or Taisen Deshimaru, whose statues reside in the Komazawa University's Museum of Zen Culture and History as examples of proper posture in zazen. In contrast to their upright strength and serenity, Rodin's *Thinker* is contorted, muscles flexed, brow furrowed, fist hard against his forehead as though he's beating himself up about something, trying to solve a problem. This might have some expressionistic parallel to Rinzai practice, but not to Soto practice.

The posture of zazen is like a mountain, rising up and settling down at the same time, comfortable with gravity yet taking its height. Snow melts downward and rocks fall, yet trees and meadows grow upward to find their natural height, and wildlife comes and goes with the seasons. One of the most majestic of Dogen's writings is the *Sansui-Kyo, or Mountains and Waters Sutra*. I return to this moving philosophical prose poem again and again, always finding some new insight in it. Dogen speaks of how "Mountains' walking is just like human walking," but we can easily substitute mountains' sitting and say it's just like human sitting. "Keeping its own form, without changing body and mind, a mountain always practices in every place." If we practice like mountains we can't go wrong. Once, after zazen, I told the group, "You all looked like mountains today, sitting erect and solid." Gary replied, "I didn't feel like a mountain. I had to keep making constant adjustments to my posture." "Even mountains," I said, "are making constant adjustments to their posture. Mountains shift, crumble, fall apart. Just like us." Unlike us, mountains don't look in the mirror and despair.

Rodin's *Thinker*, though, strives against the cosmos, against nature, feels himself to be the center of the cosmos, drawing our attention to him and his striving. This is a common Western romantic notion of heroism. The monk, as a reflection of the cosmos, goes against this individualistic notion, this self-regarding image. The monk in zazen sits neither at the center nor at the periphery but embraces and coexists interdependently with the cosmos, embodying that relationship in his posture and breathing: the posture of zazen has tension without being tense, is relaxed without being lax; the breath is natural in its intake, slow and complete in its exit, all without damaging the structure of the posture—but filling it in, emptying it out.

Sometimes we do zazen with our bodies, sometimes with our minds. Sometimes the body is willing, our posture and breathing doing just fine, but the mind is unsettled. Sometimes our mind is ready for zazen, but our bodies won't cooperate. This split, this separation of body and mind, is like two political parties—sometimes able to work together, sometimes estranged from one another. The more estranged they are, the less efficient they are, the more dysfunctional they are, the more they need zazen.

Zen practice requires determination, repetition, and letting go, so that body and mind can get back together, like old friends, and embrace, becoming one, not two. *Shin jin datsu raku.* Body and mind drop off. This is very difficult for us to understand. Body and mind dropping off, that's concentration, not unconsciousness, not a trance, not anesthetization. We might say rather that only the *"and"* of "body [and] mind" drops off so that body is concentrated in mind, and mind is concentrated in body. We say, "think with the body, act with the mind." This is Zen concentration.

Symmetry Versus Balance

Physical balance is good; psychic balance is better.

STRETCH THE BACKBONE. Don't slump. Always let your head press the sky. Your spine should be a pillar, a living pillar, always growing upward, support for your body-mind. If your spine is straight and strong, the rest of your body can relax, all the organs hanging off the spine, all the limbs at ease. If you don't feel that you are completely symmetrical in your posture, don't worry. You'll never achieve perfect symmetry, perfect posture. But you will achieve balance.

There's something to be learned from the different aesthetics of Chinese and Japanese art and literature. Chinese are always looking for symmetry, an even number of lines in their poetic stanzas, a reciprocity of action: she gives him a peach, while he gives her a gemstone. Notice that reciprocity, though, is not perfectly symmetrical either, even though it does achieve the balance demanded by justice or the sexual economy.

Japanese, on the other hand, tend to find balance through asymmetry. In *waka* poems, or haiku, you have the five lines or three lines, and always something is left out for you the reader to fill in. The reciprocity is not to be found within the poem, but outside the poem, with the reader. The poet gives you an image, or just the suggestion of an image, and expects you to fill in the blanks. Notice how flower arrangements (ikebana) are never perfectly symmetrical yet they achieve balance. Notice the martial arts, how essential the center of balance is in both Chinese and Japanese martial arts, how one side of the body moves, shifting the center of gravity, so that the other can strike out with a powerful fist or foot. This is because there is a spine, an invisible spine, bisecting the middle of the flower arrangement, the painting, the poem, the martial artist, that balances the two sides, brings their separate shapes and actions into harmony.

This is what you are doing with your zazen. The two sides of your body are not symmetrical. Always one arm is favored, one is weaker, one shoulder slumps, one thumb forces itself upon the other, one lung takes in more oxygen, one ear hears more sharply, one eye droops. But we manage to compensate for these imbalances by various means, becoming more aware of them, working on our weaknesses, playing to our strengths. These are very practical compensations, but they are also based on a perception that is primarily aesthetic.

Notice how often we find the beauty in an object to be in its asymmetry. In the faces of the ones you have fallen in love with, isn't it the crooked tooth, the unruly lock of hair, the fleck of black in one green eye that fascinates you? Too much asymmetry, it's true, can be the very definition of ugliness, but two much symmetry has the cold perfection of ice and leaves us cold.

I think you realize I am not talking so much about physical symmetry. I am not talking about the material spine, the physical backbone and vertebrae but rather what we might call the spiritual center of balance, and by spiritual I mean simply emotional and intellectual balance, aesthetic balance. Physical balance is good; emotional or spiritual balance— let's call it *psychic* balance—is better.

This is why we always say that zazen teaches us how to be. Our own body teaches us. Zazen is not an end in itself, even though it is practiced for its own sake. The simple activity of sitting with our own body-mind and observing its relationship with itself, with others, with its environment, this is our true teacher if only we are willing always to come back to that first principle that I can hear my teacher pronouncing: "Stretch the backbone; head presses the sky."

The Boy Who Loved Dragons

You are the dragon!

I SHOULD PROBABLY SPEND some time on the story about the boy who loved dragons. He surrounded himself with pictures of dragons, statues of dragons, books about dragons. One day a real dragon, flattered by all the admiration lavished upon him by the boy from afar, decided to pay the boy a visit. He popped his scaly head in the boy's window and said hello. This wonderful, impressive dragon had only to flare his nostrils and the boy fainted. Katagiri mentions this story in his *Buddhist Lay Ordination Lectures* to illustrate a point about the difference between Zen practice and mere intellectual curiosity. It is also a story about meeting ourselves.

It is a story about mistaking the finger for the moon, a story about painted rice cakes. It's a story about mountains that are not mountains, and rivers that are not rivers. It's a story about good intentions but no follow-through. It's a story about sitting on your zafu and dreaming about achieving enlightenment instead of concentrating on your posture and breathing. It's a story about imagining the beautiful experience of *kensho* or satori when suddenly your zafu sits up and says hello and you run away. It's a story about surrounding yourself with Buddhas and books about Buddhas, wrapping yourself in mala beads, but when you're faced with a breathing Buddha you faint dead away. Or, what is more likely, you fail to recognize that it is a Buddha and pass on by, intent on tasting your painted rice cakes.

It's a very simple story: the dragon is Zen practice. You can talk about it all you want. You can think about it, brag about it, dream about it, complain about it, but if you don't sit there is no Zen. No dragon, just rice cake dragons.

Right now, this talk is not zazen. My talk is another finger pointing at the moon. I'm not giving you zazen; I'm giving you the finger. If you are doing zazen, this doesn't bother you. You are a mountain, a rock, the moon, a dragon.

So don't surround yourself with books and Buddhas. Don't use your zafu for décor. Don't collect rice cake dragons. Collect yourself. You are the dragon. Do zazen. Realize that. Don't worship the Buddha, just be the Buddha. Do zazen. Be yourself. Be zazen. Do yourself.

Zazen Is an Inclusive Practice

Just sitting does not exclude anything.

ZEN PRACTICE IS VERY simple. We just sit. But don't assume that just sitting means that we just sit. Just sitting means doing whatever you are doing completely. So when we enter the dojo, we just enter the dojo. When we sit, we just sit. When we bow, we just bow. We are not striving for anything else through bowing. When we do *gassho*, we just do gassho. We are not currying favor. Just sitting does not mean not doing gassho. Just sitting does not mean not doing ceremony, although some people would have you think so. Just sitting does not mean not doing samu. Just sitting does not mean not reading and thinking. Just sitting is not an excuse for not doing anything. It is a reason for doing everything that we do completely, with our whole heart.

Just sitting does not exclude anything: it includes everything. That's why there is no reason to worry that you are missing out on something that you're not doing when you are doing zazen. By doing zazen, you are doing just one thing, not two. You are not divided, which means that you are doing everything that needs to be done. Also, when you are not doing zazen, then you can do whatever those other things are, working, reading, helping others, completely, with a whole heart.

Do you see? Zazen is not an exclusive practice; it's an inclusive practice. The emptiness you nurture with your zazen expands to embrace the world, the entire cosmos. Very simple.

Sesshin Is Not a Marathon

Returning to the source for a short while.

SESSHIN MEANS TO TOUCH the mind. But this does not mean the thinking mind, the thinking brain. We touch that enough every day. During sesshin it is the heart/mind, the body/mind that we get in touch with. Sesshin is for just this, nothing more. It's very simple; don't complicate it. Don't complicate sesshin with ideas. Sesshin is not the place to figure things out. It's not for dredging up old memories or devising agendas for the future. It's not for settling old scores or coming up with new schemes. It's for paying attention to here and now, to what is right in front of us. This is how we reconnect with the source of all thoughts, memories, and agendas. Sesshin is just like everyday Zen practice, only more so.

So keep it simple. Don't complicate things. For example, when we say that we connect with the Three Treasures, don't complicate this connection with abstractions or ideas from your reading about Buddhism. If you think the Three Treasures are Buddha, Dharma, and Sangha, then you are thinking too hard, turning them into textbook definitions, concepts, abstractions. There's no exam! You can't pass by being clever; you can pass only by embodying these concepts, by connecting with them personally, by turning abstractions into your everyday practice. The Three Treasures that have been passed down to us are simple: posture, breathing, attitude of mind.

Posture is the posture of the Buddha, nothing more, nothing less. As long as you have a stable base, whether you are sitting in seiza, or on a bench, or in one of the lotus positions, or on a chair, it doesn't matter. This posture allows you to sit with a minimum of discomfort for a long period of time. Hips tilted slightly forward, lower back slightly curved, collarbone up, chin tucked in, ears over shoulders, nose over navel, eyes cast down at a 45-degree angle, head pressing the sky. This is simply the embodiment of the emptiness of the Buddha. Let your posture speak for you.

Breathing is the Dharma, both natural and necessary; without it, nothing. Don't complicate the Dharma by turning it into philosophy, rules, fancy words and phrases. Breathe deep into the hara, allowing your lungs to fill up, all the way down and into your back. Then let the air out in long slow, deep exhalations. This is the Dharma at work, it is yin and yang, it is "form is emptiness, emptiness is form." Learn from it. Let your breath be your teacher.

Attitude of mind is the Sangha. Don't make the mistake of thinking that attitude of mind has to do with what you think or how you feel. It's not about you. It has to do with others, with those of us practicing here today, with others who are not here today, with all practitioners, with all people, and with all beings, all existences. When you practice with the right attitude of mind, it is not about what you do or don't do; it is not about you. Mushotoku mind, the mind of no profit, no personal gain, is the attitude of practicing for its own sake, not for what it will do, not for any outcome. This is the source of peace, the mind that is unobstructed. Let your mind let go of all intention.

This is what sesshin is: touching the mind that without intention achieves the benefit of all others, touching the breath that breathes for all others, touching the posture that is the posture of all others. Returning to the source for a short while. Not difficult. Not easy. Just pay attention.

Some people will inevitably compare sesshin to a marathon. But this is not right. Sesshin is a little training sprint for the marathon that is your life's practice. After sesshin is when the real work begins.

On Attachment

Clinging

We cling to things that appear to cling to us.

THERE'S A STORY IN the *Vimalakirti Nirdesa Sutra* about clinging to things, clinging to what we might or might not like. A group of bodhisattvas and the Buddha's chief disciples are gathered in Vimalakirti's room. A celestial maiden, eavesdropping, flies overhead and showers them with a basketful of flower petals. The petals drift down and settle on their robes, then slide off, not finding anything to cling to. Shariputra, the Buddha's cleverest disciple (and foil of the *Heart Sutra*), tries to shake off the flowers and cannot. "The petals are clinging to my robes but not to anyone else's. Why is that?" The celestial creature looks down and says, "It's not the petals that are clinging to your robes, but you who are clinging to the petals."

This story explains how we cling to things that appear to cling to us. Shariputra is clinging to pleasant things, but the maiden might as well have dropped buckets of garbage on the group with the same effect. The garbage would have clung to some, not to the bodhisattvas. It would not have been the garbage clinging to them, but them clinging to the garbage. It's like our thoughts. It's not our thoughts that trouble us, but we who allow ourselves to be troubled by our thoughts. Zazen teaches us that these thoughts have no substantial reality. It's not that they don't exist, but they have no substance, no lasting identity, no metaphysical reality. In zazen we find—connect to—something substantial, even though that reality is emptiness (ku) and constant change (mujo).

Mujo and Karma

Zazen cuts karma, minimizes mujo.

IT'S WORTH CONSIDERING the relationship between mujo (constant change) and karma (cause and effect). We often separate those two, think about them one at a time, as though they were discrete events or processes, even though they are intimately entwined, intricately involved with one another—if we think about them in an exact way. But first we need to strip karma of the idea of a metaphysical system of justice, reward and punishment. This is only the ego's small way of interpreting karma: does this cause-and-effect chain benefit or punish me or others that I know? This is just karma with a small k. Karma stripped of such divine or religious intention is much more all-pervasive, disinterested, scientific. Our problem of course is that we always interpret causes by their effects so we have a very limited idea of the vast nature of causes that are always much more complex than our minds can grasp, so we seek meaning in effects and cling to these simplistic interpretations.

Mujo similarly. The kind of mujo that comes down to us in the form of a small m comes from the capriciousness of individuals. It certainly has an effect on us. But if we have trust—trust in mind, *shinjinmei*—it has very little effect on our equanimity, our ability to deal with whatever comes to us. Certainly, though, that kind of mujo can have dire effects, random shootings, crimes. But if we look at the intricate causes that go into such things we see that it all comes from suffering. It results in suffering but it comes from suffering as well. Mujo with a big M, that's the constant change that we never get away from; we can never find the cause of it, or the effect, or the reason why it occurs.

This is why zazen is so important. Zazen cuts karma, minimizes mujo. It aligns our interpretation of events with reality, not with our personal preference for how things should be. Mujo, karma, finally they're just words—big M, little m, big K, little k—just words for a mystery. With zazen we sit in the middle of that mystery, don't have to figure it out: the mystery figures us out. This is why we come back to the four noble truths of suffering, the causes of suffering, ways to relieve suffering through concentration, daily attention to the epiphenomena of mujo and karma. Zen practice is not metaphysics, it's just everyday life.

Don't Become Attached to Attachment

Attachment is a very shallow emotion.

ONE OF YOU ASKED, "I want to ask about attachment. I have difficulty understanding non-attachment because I feel we need to be very attached to some things and to enjoy them and to suffer when we lose them because they may be sublime."

Don't mistake enjoyment or suffering for attachment. You're attached to your arm. If your arm becomes unattached, you're going to suffer. If you don't feel pain, you're a monster. You take pleasure in your children's accomplishments, or you enjoy a hike in the woods or a work of art. Some forms of attachment are natural. You're emotionally attached to your children—that's natural—and if you're not, you're a monster. That's not attachment, that's emotion, that's feeling, that's being human. Just don't become attached to your attachment. Being attached to your attachment is unnatural, it's unhealthy, it's neurotic, and you can harm your children by being attached to your attachment to them.

Non-attachment in the Buddhist sense doesn't mean you can't become involved in things; it doesn't mean you float around above the ground like some superior being. On the contrary. You're very much involved and you're part of the world, but that's not attachment, that's involvement, that's activity, that's feeling, that's emotion, and all those things are great. But if you're attached to your attachment you won't let your children leave when they grow up, you won't let them get out of your sight to go play in the yard: that's neurosis, that's attachment. You're afraid something's going to happen to them and you're going to lose them and you become overprotective. You suffer, and they suffer.

Non-attachment is very difficult for us in the West to understand. What it doesn't mean is not feeling. You need to be attached to your kids. You should even be attached to your ambitions if you want to become really good at something. Let's say you want to be an astronaut, though, and you don't have what it takes. It's better if you can detach yourself from that ambition and find another career path. Stalkers have attachment problems; they can't take no for an answer. Hoarders have attachment issues; unable to bear having lost something, they become attached to everything they come in contact with, including their own garbage.

Attachment disorder is primarily an identity disorder. Someone who commits suicide because they wrecked their Mercedes is attached to their Mercedes. They're not just attached to the pleasure of strapping themselves in for a luxurious ride. They have become so attached to the idea of having a Mercedes that their identity has become confused with it, so when the car crashes so do they. They don't own the Mercedes, the Mercedes owns them. Same thing if you are too attached to your kids; you don't want them to own you.

If you become too identified with your job and you lose it, you lose everything because you lose yourself. But take Beethoven: do you think he was attached to music? Of course he was. He loved music more than his own life. But why then when he went deaf did he not despair? Because he was not attached to the sound of music. Even though he couldn't hear the sound, he could hear the music in his head, so he kept on composing. In this sense he was not attached to his attachment to music. Attachment is really a very shallow emotion. Beethoven's involvement in music was deeper than that. Our important relationships, such as those with our kids, should be much deeper, much more profound than mere attachment.

Nothing for Something

In Zen practice, you don't get something for nothing.

MUSHOTOKU. THIS IS OUR ATTITUDE of mind when we practice. It means "no profit, no personal gain." This is a big stumbling block for some people. It is very difficult to understand why we practice without some sense of short-term or long-term profit. Yet it is the very practice of seeking after profit and gain that stresses us out and makes us look for something like zazen. Mushotoku, though, is not an escape from profit and gain. It is not a rejection. It is simply a recognition that there is a state of mind in which profit and gain play no part. Very few Zen teachers in the West ever mention it. In the Deshimaru lineage mushotoku takes center stage. Yet if we look back into the Zen literature, or even look at our own experience, it is clear that without mushotoku mind there is no real Zen practice.

There are many ways to misunderstand mushotoku. One way is to ask yourself: "Why do it if I'm not going to get anything out of it?" That's pretty common. Another way is to ask the Zen center: "Why do you charge if you're not looking for profit?" Zen centers always require some sort of payment. They might call it a donation, or *fuse* (open hand, generosity). This fuse is more for the giver than for the Zen center or temple. People come looking to get something for nothing. They feel entitled for some reason. Religion, they say, is supposed to be free. I've never known anyone who came to zazen expecting to get something for free who could actually practice, who had the discipline to practice. The fuse is a token of one's seriousness. It doesn't have to be much, but it must be tangible. This is because in Zen practice you don't get something for nothing. In fact, you get nothing for something. But this nothing is precisely the point. This nothing is of great value, the greatest value.

Traditionally, when you came to enter the Zen monastery you would have to stand outside in the cold, one day, two days, three days; only then they might let you in, but they would only let you into the waiting room. You might have to stay quite a while there, too. This let you demonstrate that you had the determination to practice. Nowadays, though, Zen centers will go to great lengths to proselytize, designing attractive websites, placing expensive ads in the Buddhist magazines. No one is made to wait in the cold, no one is told to go away. The message is just the opposite: come to us, we will accommodate you, we will make it easy for you to practice.

A couple of stories about Bodhidharma, the first Zen patriarch, are relevant. One is that his disciple, Huike, the one who became his successor, came to the monastery, where he waited outside the door, was rejected, waited and was rejected. Only when he cut off his right arm and offered that as fee and proof of his earnestness was he admitted entrance. His fuse was quite literally an open hand.

There is also a story about the Emperor Wu who came to Bodhidharma and asked about how much merit he had acquired in building Buddhist temples. He spent a lot of money, he even practiced with Bodhidharma, but when he wanted Bodhidharma to certify that he had accomplished something, Bodhidharma refused. The Emperor said, "Don't

I get anything for everything I gave to the temple? Isn't there any merit in that?" Bodhidharma was clear: "No merit. Vast emptiness." Not that the Emperor hadn't done a fine thing, it's just that doing fine things doesn't have anything to do with Zen practice, especially if one expects to get something in return.

So when we say that Zen practice is not easy, not difficult, this idea of mushotoku mind arises. You don't have to give much materially, but you have to give all your determination. You have to give up all of your expectations. All you get in return is everything.

Every Zazen Is Unique

"Who is this 'I' who says 'my'?"

EVERY ZAZEN IS UNIQUE. Not just different from the time before, but unique, incomparable, unrepeatable. This is one reason we keep the basic structure of the dojo consistent—the shape, the arrangement, the times and days, the process of entering and exiting, the direction we sit, the sequence in which we bow, the temperature, the lighting, the incense, the ceremony—not because we're looking for some perfect order or because the order is significant but because this allows us to recognize the subtle changes that happen each time we sit. It can never be the same. The way the gong is struck never sounds the same way twice. The ceremony always has its glitches.

I remember well the times my master would forget the chant that he'd chanted for thirty years. Once, as he was about to signal the end of zazen, he accidentally flung the striker of the gong halfway across the room. These unique moments or "errors" are instructive. Nobody's perfect; but every moment *is* perfect. Incomparable.

Even people who have practiced for quite some time fall into comparing one zazen with another. "Oooh, today was a good zazen," or "Today was a bad zazen." There's no such thing. You may have enjoyed it more, or you may not have enjoyed it as much. Maybe your mind was racing or your body was at ease. But that's just your discriminating mind, your delusion. It's best to pay as little attention as possible to the differences between this zazen and that zazen, because once you start making value judgments between this zazen and that zazen, they never end. This is what gets us caught up in our clever, ceaseless mind games that go on and on.

Sometimes people who have practiced for years might fall into talking about "my practice," or "my zazen," as though it were different than someone else's. And it is different, but the difference isn't what's important, it's the uniqueness that's important, and what is unique is by definition incomparable. As soon as you say "my" zazen, "my" practice, as though you own it, you betray your practice, you put your ego on display. The very practice of zazen, the very experience of zazen should teach us to ask: *"Who is this 'I' who says 'my'?"* This 'I' is not really substantial, and so you can't really own a practice, you can't really own a zazen; you can just barely own your own identity for a short period of time.

This problem of locating a substantial identity is one of the reasons why each of our zazens is unique: we sit down a different person each time. We all know this theoretically— we're a little older, we've shed some cells, replaced a few. But we really are different; our experience has changed us, moment to moment. As Heraclitus might say, we never sit on the same zafu twice, or more relevantly, a zafu is never sat upon by the same person twice. If we learn nothing else in zazen it should be this. Dogen said, "To study the self is to forget the self." Dogen always cuts both ways with his statements, so the reverse of what he says is also true: to forget the self is to study the self. This is what we do in zazen.

It's like a coin flipping over. First we see our face on one side of the coin, our reflection in the mirror of our mind— this is to study the self. Then we flip it over and we see our original face before our parents were born—this is to forget the self. Form is emptiness: emptiness is form.

When we first sit down in zazen, we are probably studying ourselves, observing ourselves, observing our mind, thinking about our past and our future, our present. This studying of the self becomes a forgetting of the self. By concentrating on the self completely we are not really grasping after anything; it's a form of desire perhaps, but it's not so invidious, not so bad, not so harmful—it doesn't create a lot of bad karma. Then, there comes a point in zazen when you go from studying the self (primarily) to forgetting the self (primarily), but then to forget the self is to study the self—even more deeply.

Sometimes during zazen you might do a little more forgetting the self. Sometimes you might do a little more studying the self. But remember, it's the same thing, so don't judge yourself. Don't say, "I didn't do so well today. I couldn't control my mind. I was full of delusions." Even more important, don't say to yourself, "I did pretty darn good today. I had satori." Just do it. Just sit. No self-flagellation, no self-congratulation, no self whatsoever.

Then you'll get a greater sense of calm, a greater sense of fulfillment than with the small distinction that can be put into words, that sort of discrimination that relies on comparison, that puny pleasure that comes from putting yourself down or puffing yourself up, comparing yourself with others or even with yourself. There's nothing to be accomplished here, no transformation of consciousness; we're not trying to achieve anything but to be here and now, in this unique moment, this zazen.

Zazen Makes Nothing Happen

After we've walked through the stream, the mud settles.

THE POET W. H. AUDEN said, "Poetry makes nothing happen." On one level this is just a statement of art for art's sake. We can't expect poetry to accomplish anything in the world. On another level it's more interesting; because if poetry makes nothing happen, then it brings nothing into existence. It makes nothing *happen.*

We tend to think of peace not as *nothing* happening but as something tranquil happening: nature's pastoral, streams burbling, and most of all our being conscious of witnessing tranquility happening. So usually when we feel tranquil, when we're conscious of being tranquil, we have to be doing something to be tranquil: we have a picnic or take a walk. We set out to be tranquil, and sometimes we cause a big to-do in the process. Sometimes, it turns out to be not so tranquil. Just going out of the house to discover our peace gets us in trouble. It's difficult to do nothing, to be at peace.

Another way of thinking about nothing happening is that when there's peace no karma is being created, no cause and effect is being put into motion. After we've walked through the stream, the mud settles. Not that the stream doesn't keep flowing, it's just that it goes back to its original state.

Zazen is like this. Zazen makes nothing happen.

Zazen Won't Make You a Better Person

All I mean by the truth is the path I have to travel.
—Oliver Wendell Holmes

WE OFTEN SAY THAT zazen won't make you a better person. Of course, this isn't strictly true. Because if zazen can do what we say it can do, the result might well be a better person, depending on what we mean by "better" and depending on what we mean by "person." What we mean by this seemingly negative statement—"zazen won't make you a better person"—is that you can't go into your practice relying on zazen to solve your problems. If you do, there will be no result at all.

One of the things that zazen can do is to increase our awareness of exactly what our problems are. So if we have imbalances in the body, we become aware of them. Our bodies are inscriptions of karma, no less than our minds. The more we study the body by concentrating, by becoming aware of our breathing, by observing our posture, we can't help but become aware of our imbalances. And with awareness, with cognition, the more likely we are to change.

Most of this change, however, is unconscious. This is why we make no rules about diet, meat, alcohol, sugar. Usually, when people are sitting regularly, they become so aware of how their bodies are reacting to meat, sugar, alcohol, they make their own adjustments. They tend to eat less meat, drink less alcohol, walk with better posture, sit up straighter. These natural, unconscious adjustments have beneficial consequences—not just physically but emotionally and mentally. As we become aware of our emotional imbalances, psychic imbalances, these too become part of the study of the self, part of the unconscious activity of the inner reconstruction that is the natural and spontaneous work of zazen.

Over time, in my own practice, I haven't solved all my problems, certainly not. Problems are part of everyday life and never stop. "Delusions are endless," says one of the bodhisattva vows; "I vow to drop them all." Getting up every morning, sitting through every zazen, keeping up the practice, creates a rhythm, an attitude of determination that can be applied to any situation, any problem. That doesn't mean that practicing zazen will make you successful in confronting those problems always, but the benefits of your increased awareness, your ability to concentrate, can't be discounted.

In my own practice, too, I find that I'm not necessarily a happier person, not necessarily a sadder person, certainly not a better person. But somehow when a great happiness comes, I am simultaneously more aware of the great sadness everywhere, the great sadness that underpins every great upsurge of joy. Likewise, when I'm sad or depressed, it's not total depression, because I'm simultaneously aware of the great undercurrent of joy that buoys up that sadness. Without the oceanic joy that's underneath the great burden of the sadness of the world, it would all simply sink.

This, I think, is all we really mean when we talk about compassion. It's no longer "my" sadness or "my" joy, but my sadness rises up on the tide of the world's joy; my joy is borne up on the swell of the world's sadness. And so we cease to feel special or isolated in either our sadness or our joy, but rather we begin to feel with all beings. When we chant the first bodhisattva vow—*shujo muhen seigan do*: "I vow to save all beings however numberless, however many there are"—this is the great promise that rises on the tide of the great failure: the boy on the ox, the monkey on the dragon, the cork on the sea.

So what we mean when we say that zazen will not make you a better person is that it won't make you a better social being, more acceptable, more successful, nicer. It will, however, make you a better human being, one that feels this greater undercurrent of reality of which your minute emotional ebbs and flows are tributaries. It's what I suppose my master means when he says that zazen allows us to "follow the cosmic order," naturally, unconsciously, automatically.

There's No Koan Like a Corpse

This is what it means to sit in emptiness.

ZAZEN IS NOT FOR working on your problems. You should be working only on your posture and breathing. Problems will arise during zazen while you are paying attention to your posture and breathing. Problems will arise and distract you, disrupting your concentration. Don't follow the problems though. Follow your breath instead. Don't push the problem out of your mind, set it down beside you. You might have heard someone talk about "sitting with a problem." This comes from the Rinzai tradition of "sitting with" a koan. It does not mean that you try to figure it out by thinking about it. The rational mind is not a useful tool for cracking a koan. Instead, you sit with a koan as you would sit with another person in the dojo. Set the problem down beside you but don't try to solve it, just sit with it. Your problems are just another member of the sangha. Harmonize with them as you would the person on the zafu next to you.

You may have heard of the tradition of sitting zazen with corpses. You should sit with your problems as you would sit with a corpse. Corpses are a particular kind of koan, very powerful koans. When someone dies, we naturally confront the great matter of life and death, and of course there are no good answers; there are only more or less useful ways of dealing with the great matter. You can't solve a corpse as you might solve an everyday problem. You must go through a series of thoughts and emotions and reactions when confronted with a corpse, and you do something similar with any problem. Problems are corpses. They can only be buried at the proper time.

Sitting with problems is only helpful when you sit without goal, without object, with mushotoku mind, without even the goal of attaining "mindfulness" or compassion. In zazen we sit within emptiness, allowing the problem to reveal itself for what it is, as unsubstantial, as "not here and now." This is what it means to sit in emptiness. Then your unconscious can work on the problem, zazen can work on the problem through the primal parts of the brain, so that you can return to the problem with a new awareness when you step out of the dojo. Don't expect to solve or dissolve the problem in the dojo. The problem will be waiting for you outside, but you will be better equipped to deal with it because of what zazen has been doing with it and with you. You will be better able to deal with the problem spontaneously, naturally, automatically because you sat with it beside you instead of confronting it head on as though you were master of it, as though you were so clever that you thought you could think your way through it. Zazen is not clever, it is wise. And wisdom is always better than cleverness.

Don't Hold Your Breath

People will wait forever for Daruma's second coming.

BODHIDHARMA IS CALLED THE FIRST Zen patriarch, the one who brought *dhyana* Buddhism, or Zen, to China from the West, from India. Quite a few koans, stories and legends are associated with Bodhidharma, called Ta Mo in Chinese and Daruma in Japanese. One of the most famous koans is the question, "Why did Bodhidharma come from the West?" The answer is always something like "The oak tree in the garden."

Various legends sprung up around him. Some appear to be true, like his establishing the Shaolin monastery in China, and he may have been the originator of martial arts as a way of keeping the monks active in between meditation sessions. He probably did not cut off his eyelids, though, to stay awake during his nine years of meditating in a cave. And the first tea leaves in China almost certainly did not spring from his eyelids when they hit the ground, although it's a pretty story. Cutting off his eyelids would certainly help to keep him awake, and the caffeine in tea might have had a similar effect through less drastic means. He has inspired some interesting myths.

Daruma is often depicted in hanging scrolls like the two hanging in the dojo during this sesshin, one behind me and one over the altar. These *sumi-e*, very quick ink drawings can be cartoonish. Daruma often looks like Homer Simpson, although he can also look very stern. Monks or artists trained in Zen painting (*zenga*) often add calligraphy as a caption to emphasize one of the many aspects of Zen practice that Daruma has come to represent, especially the equal standing of all buddhas everywhere and the necessity for determination in Zen practice.

In Japan, Daruma is especially associated with children and prostitutes. He is a favorite subject for toys, especially those dolls that are weighted on the bottom so that no matter how many times you push them over they always spring back up. It is a good object lesson for children and prostitutes, too—that you can't be knocked over if you maintain your balance. He is sometimes depicted in the clothing of a prostitute, suggesting that there is nothing pure or impure. The calligraphy on the scroll behind me says: "All beings are equal with the Buddha." Bodhidharma and the Buddha are the same. You and I and Bodhidharma and Buddha are the same. Children and prostitutes and Bodhidharma and the Buddha are all the same. All equal.

He also has come to represent determination. This is probably the most common association with Bodhidharma: "Don't give up!" There is a fierce urgency to the practice, not like the Buddha of India, who is all calmness and compassion. Influenced by Taoism, in China he became Ta Mo, a hard-ass, a taskmaster, a drill sergeant who could inspire his disciple Huike to cut off his right arm to show his determination. When he gets to Japan, he is influenced by their warrior traditions of bushido and the samurai. The scroll over the altar says something like, "People will wait forever for the second coming of Bodhidharma." In other words, you only get one chance. Don't hesitate. You only get one chance to parry the sword of your enemy, so don't hesitate. There is no second coming of Bodhidharma. Don't wait. If you are waiting for someone to come along and show you the way, you are deluded. The oak tree is already in the garden.

Daruma is depicted in a few typical ways in the scrolls. One type is a little round figure like the doll, sitting. Many depictions show him in three-quarters torso, just shoulders and head (his arms and legs are said to have fallen off during his nine years of sitting facing a wall at Shaolin). Another type has him standing, moving forward, robes flowing, crossing a river. Sometimes you can see the water flowing under his feet, especially in older, nineteenth-century Chinese depictions. He is ferrying himself across the river on a branch, coming to us perhaps, or taking us with him.

Sometimes you can see in his robes a hidden kanji, or character. In this scroll it is the character *mu*, emptiness. This could be the answer to the question of when the second coming of Bodhidharma will be. The answer is *mu*: not, no, *ain't gonna happen*. At the very bottom, instead of his feet, there is a very small *enso*, or circle, symbol of emptiness. So don't hold your breath.

Even though these drawings seem to be quickly drawn, dashed off very lightly, there is much more going on than it seems at first. Zazen is like this too. There doesn't seem to be much to it from the outside. But the more we sit, the more we find, the clearer it becomes.

That doesn't mean we don't have doubts about whether we can keep it up, or even why we keep it up. If we didn't have doubts, there would be no reason for Bodhidharma to sit up there frowning and saying: "Stick with it!" Like Homer Simpson, though, Daruma is also a reminder not to take it all too seriously, not to take it too lightly. Balance!

Change and Balance

Everything is available to us here and now.

WHEN SHUNRYU SUZUKI WAS asked for one word to describe Zen, he said, "Change." The word we use for this is mujo, constant change.

The word the Romantic poets liked to use was "Mutability," the title of a poem by Shelley that begins:

> *We are as clouds that veil the midnight moon;*
> *How restlessly they speed, and gleam, and quiver,*
> *Streaking the darkness radiantly!—yet soon*
> *Night closes round, and they are lost forever.*

In Zen practice we need to be aware that even when things don't seem to be changing there is the potential for abrupt, sudden, radical change. Things are constantly changing under our eyes, under our noses, with or without our perception of them. The more we practice, the more attentive we become to the subtle universe of change occurring in and around us, to the real change occurring every moment, and to the vast potential for drastic change within every next moment.

Zen practice is about balance in the midst of change. During zazen we sit in a posture of balance within the streams of change. Balance might look at first glance to have little to do with change, it may look to some like an attempt to forestall change, or the very opposite of change, but in fact change *is* balance. When we try to keep things from changing, when we don't adjust to the always changing circumstances, that's when our life gets out of balance. Imagine riding a mountain-bike over rough terrain: how long would you stay upright without shifting with the landscape, constantly changing your balance to adjust to the second-by-second situation under your wheels? When we cling to the way things are, the way they have been, or the way we would like them to be, that's what throws us off. But we have to find a way to respond spontaneously and automatically to the changing situation because if we think too much about riding a bike, we will fall off for sure. We just ride.

So one of the things to be attentive to in our practice is our response to change: when to initiate change, and how to respond to change. When you come to zazen, for example, you are initiating an action. When you don't come to zazen, you are also initiating an action. Either way, things will change as a result of your action. It's your choice. During zazen, as you sit on your zafu, you learn the appropriate response to everything that is changing in your body, in your mind. You learn that every zazen is unique and that no two responses to zazen can be the same.

As Shelley says, "We are as clouds,"

> *Or like forgotten lyres, whose dissonant strings*
> *Give various response to each varying blast,*
> *To whose frail frame no second motion brings*
> *One mood or modulation like the last.*

Change is really balance. Without change, no balance.

The *Heart Sutra* says, form is emptiness, emptiness is form; form becomes emptiness, emptiness becomes form. This is a precise description of how change becomes balance, and balance becomes change. During zazen you can feel the process in your breath, you can feel it in the contractions and relaxations of your muscles, you can see it in the changes in your mental landscape as the minutes pass. Normally, though, whether we are asleep or awake, we tend to see things according to how they affect us and our preferences, fears, and desires, and so these changes appear to be threatening, and they are because they toss us back and forth. Again, Shelley puts it well:

> We rest. —A dream has power to poison sleep;
> We rise. —One wandering thought pollutes the day;
> We feel, conceive or reason, laugh or weep;
> Embrace fond woe, or cast our cares away.

When Suzuki identified Zen with change, he wasn't just saying that change is a lens through which Zen looks at the world, but that through our practice we attend to the world moment by moment, just as it is: constantly changing. Attending to that change, then, is simply to be aware of our being in the world. Change is the way we are in the world, the way we are in time. Change is how we "be" in time.

Or as Shelley puts it, ending the poem:

> It is the same!—For, be it joy or sorrow,
> The path of its departure still is free:
> Man's yesterday may ne'er be like his morrow;
> Nought may endure but Mutability.

Shelley states the situation very well; he has no answer, though, for how to meet or defeat Mutability. Indeed, Mutability, or mujo, cannot be defeated. He comes close to an answer in noting that the "path" of the departure of joy or sorrow "still is free."

Our awareness that there is nothing *but* Change lends an urgency to our practice. Not the kind of urgency that causes us to pack our lives with activity as though we are afraid of missing out on something (much as Shelley did in his short, fevered life, it seems), but the kind of urgency that makes us realize that we are already experiencing everything here and now. Everything is available to us here and now. This is the urgency of practicing *as though our hair is on fire*. This doesn't mean that you run around trying to put the fire out. It means that you sit calmly with an awareness that life is short, time is brief, and you should therefore be ready when change comes, when mujo strikes—ready to act or not to act, as the occasion demands.

You can count on this: that mujo will strike. Everything will be different tomorrow. Don't waste your time. Keep things in balance. The best way to keep things in balance is to do zazen. Zazen is the physical and mental embodiment of balance. You can always come back to zazen. Zazen will always be there. Zazen doesn't change. Zazen *is* change.

Tathata: The The

Q: What is Tathata?
A: The The.

THERE USED TO BE a TV show in the late '50s, early
'60s, called *This Is Your Life*. They would bring celebrities
and surprise them with a spotlight on their life. They would
bring in people they had known from their past who would
give anecdotes, stories about the person, creating a mini-
documentary on the celebrity, a biography seen through the
eyes of others.

Sometimes we think this kind of narrative really is our
life. We think that the narratives others have created for
us, or even the ones we create for ourselves, are who we
are. The stories become us, our biography becomes us, our
autobiography becomes us. When a narrative takes our place,
instead of a life we have literature—or caricature—a kind of
demonic possession.

But that isn't your life. *This* is your life, what's happening
right now, here and now, always here and now. It's not the
sum total of your experience: it's not your curriculum vitae.
That's your karma, not your life.

There's a wonderful poem by Wislawa Szymborska, the
Nobel Prize winning Polish poet, called "Writing a Curriculum
Vitae." It talks about how when we write a CV we only put
those things in that will sell us, so that when we are applying
for a job, for example, we put in only the loves that resulted
in marriage, the children that were born, destinations not

journeys, and so on. "Write as if you never talked with yourself, / as if you looked at yourself from afar." We put down what creates the impression of "the one you are supposed to be." What is the sound of the totality of this portrait, the totality of this life of yours? Szymborska says: it's the sound of a machine shredding paper.

When we do zazen that is the sound we hear: the sound of shredding paper. We shred the paper of our curriculum vitae. We deconstruct all that and allow it to drop away into the garbage bin, into the trash.

All the representations of who we are, are just representations, not the reality. In Buddhism, the reality is sometimes called *tathata*, or suchness. Suchness doesn't mean much; it's a hard concept because it is not really a concept at all; it is just a word to point to an experience, and not even to an experience, but to a reality that cannot be both experienced and expressed. So it's difficult to say what suchness is. Suchness is just "as it is," not the way it's conceived, not the way it's represented, not the way the story is told, not the narrative, the anecdote, the documentary, the TV show.

This reminds me of another poem, one by Wallace Stevens called "The Man on the Dump." It's a beautiful poem about how all the things in our lives that accumulate finally get tossed out in the garbage. These things—or rather what they represent—have so much meaning, they seem so indispensable until finally they're tossed out. And if we don't toss them out during our lives, then someone else will toss them out when we're dead and their significance has evaporated.

All these things get tossed into the same dump, a sort of universal tip of images. Stevens seems to gloat about this just a little: "Ho, ho . . .," he guffaws, "The dump is full / of images." Not real things but their images. There is no suchness in the dump, only discarded items, representations emptied of meaning, emptied too of actuality. All the scientific papers about the moon are there, all the artworks about the moon, all the poems about the moon, they all get cast off into the dump.

Then, at the poem's end, Stevens does a wonderful thing. He has the actual moon rise up over the dump, and that's when

> *Everything is shed; and the moon comes up as the moon*
> *(All its images are in the dump) and you see*
> *As a man (not like an image of a man),*
> *You see the moon rise in the empty sky.*

Stevens doesn't stop there, though. This is not a Japanese poem, which would be content to suggest that at this point enlightenment has occurred and would avoid any further explanation; it's a Wallace Stevens poem, philosophical as well as lyrical, so it is fearless in posing the difficult questions so that we can provide the predicate. "Is it peace, / Is it a philosopher's honeymoon, one finds / On the dump?" What is it, exactly? Does it shut us up or inspire us, as it inspires Stevens, to say such things (attempting to express their suchness in new combinations of words) as "invisible priest" or "aptest eve"? Does it cause us to "cry stanza my stone"?

Stevens wants to interpret his own poem to us, just so we'll understand as well as feel the profound meaning of this poem. He wants us to realize that even here he is resorting, in some sense, to cliché, with his moon-poem, so he has to erase the word, show the emptiness in the form, the form in the emptiness. So he ends by asking us a question, and it's a most important question: "When was it one first heard of the truth? The the."

What is the truth? It's "the the." This "truth" is the reality beyond the representation, the antecedent behind the referent, the tathata at the source of the cliché. In a word, "the the." In Zen terms, Stevens captures the gap between *being present* (as a man, not the image of a man, apprehending the moon, not the image of the moon) and *representation* (all the images in the dump).

"The" is, of course, grammatically, *the definite article*, which is an idiomatic way of saying "the real thing." Stevens seems to be asking what it is that creeps up above all the clichés, rises above all those representations? It is the definite article, the real thing, the tathata.

I don't know if Wallace Stevens knew of Myoe's famous poem about the moon, but he might have. It goes like this:

> *Aka aka ya*
> *Aka aka aka ya*
> *Aka aka ya*
> *Aka aka aka ya*
> *Aka aka on tsuki!*

Or in English:

> *Bright bright ah*
> *Bright bright bright ah*
> *Bright bright ah*
> *Bright bright bright ah*
> *Bright bright, oh, the moon!*

It's difficult not to hear Myoe's penultimate "oh" echoed in Stevens's guffawing "Ho ho!" Each is reduced to an exhalation articulating an "oh," a "ho ho!", an "ah" or an "aha!" That's the way it is when we experience ineffable suchness, the definite article, the real thing, *the the*.

This is what we practice here and now in the dojo, in zazen. It's the sound of a more or less articulate exhalation, the sound of shedding images that fill the universal dump; it's the sound of shredding paper portraits; it's the snow of static on a '50s TV; it's the moon creeping up. This is your life. This is what Zen practice is about: realizing *the the*.

Zazen Is Being-Time

Q: Dogen says that time never arrives and therefore it never passes. Can you elaborate on that?

YES, I CAN ELABORATE on it. I'm not sure I can elucidate it.

The way we normally see things is dualistically. This is very useful. This is how language works, through difference; this is how critical thinking works, through dissection and discernment; this is how judgment occurs, through discrimination. A lot can depend on our ability to think dualistically, to tell the difference between the raw and the cooked, what is healthy and what is unhealthy, what is right and what is wrong, what is beautiful and what is ugly. Our survival depends on this, procreation, aesthetic enjoyment, not just the primal concerns but also those that we think of as refined, almost everything, in fact, in our daily lives. This includes our sense of time, which is a very useful fiction. Looking back on what has happened in the past, planning for what is to come, thinking about these in contrast to the present moment. The creation of time, the creation of a past and the creation of a future have been very useful for us, but we have to remember that these exist only in our minds. God didn't need to create the world, he only needed to create time. The rest was up to us.

Dogen talks about Being-Time or Time-Being. Notice that he puts the words together into one. Time and Being are identical in a continuous present. No past, no future, only time being.

In the West we have had a lot of philosophers who have tackled this problem of time and being. Sartre in *L'Être et le Néant* (*Being and Nothingness*), Heidegger in *Sein und Zeit* (*Being and Time*), Bergson in *Durée et simultanéité* (*Duration and Simultaneity*). It's said that Bergson, examining our experience of time against Einstein's relativity theory, didn't know enough advanced mathematics or physics to make a strong case. People who study this kind of thing say that Heidegger is the closest thing to Dogen on this matter of Being-Time, Being and Time. Maybe so. But there is still a pronounced dualism in Sartre and Heidegger. Sartre talks about how Being is a sort of solid block of existence, like matter except that it can't be called matter because it is not differentiated, not distinguishable from anything else. In the beginning there is being, in the end there is being; before we are born and after we die, being. But while we're alive there is nothingness. Our consciousness creates nothingness through a radical act of negativity (this is not that), or duality. Our consciousness creates a crack in Being, opens up a gap so that we can embrace being. Think of your consciousness as a gaping hole or a window; when it sees something, senses something, these things fill it up, like a picture frame. You can also see nothingness (*le Néant*) as a light penetrating the darkness of undifferentiated Being (*L'Être*).

In this connection I am always reminded of the hilarious lecture on time from Alain Tanner's film, *Jonah Who Will Be 25 in the Year 2000* (1976). It is a classic scene, just five minutes long, in which a substitute history professor covers several conceptions of time over the course of human history with the assistance not of a PowerPoint but of a suitcase full of props including a meat cleaver and a string of blood sausages (his father, he says, was a butcher). In the course of the lecture he manages to mention Darwin, Marx, Einstein, Diderot, Freud, and Rousseau. At the end of the lecture, he has the students thump out a "binary rhythm like the heart" on their desks, gradually increasing the tempo until "in a total synthesis time disappears!"

In a sense we see that same rhythm of the human heart tapping out shiki (form or phenomena) and ku (consciousness or emptiness) because we know that although they are perceived as two beats, they are really the same, one becoming the other in a rapidly increasing acceleration (not unlike the alternating accelerations of the *han* and the *umpan* before breakfast, or the inkin and the gong during ceremony). They are really the same, one becoming the other, the other becoming the one, so they are not separate.

So when Dogen says that time never arrives and therefore can never pass, he isn't saying that time doesn't exist—it does exist as a construction that is useful to us. But in reality there is only Being-Time, or Time as Being. But we spend so much time out of our present moment, out of our own Being-Time, we don't know how to exist in the Time-Being. We check our agendas, we check our emails, make plans, chew on regrets, instead of just getting over ourselves and just being here and now.

This elaboration probably doesn't help a bit. But by doing zazen you should be able to find out a little more about what Dogen meant. Because zazen is Being-Time.

Reading

Read with your body; sit with your mind.

SOME OF YOU HAVE asked me about reading. What should you read? How much should you read? How seriously should you take your reading? Is reading really necessary? Will reading hurt your practice? And so on.

Reading is fine: good books about Zen, bad books about Zen, it doesn't matter. You will do what you need to do with these books. But don't bring your reading into the dojo; bring the dojo to your reading. You ask me if this or that is a good book. I could tell you my opinion—but that wouldn't do you any good. It wouldn't do me any good, either. But if you take your zazen to your reading, you can check what you are reading with the truth of your own experience, your own practice, your own sitting. Use your zazen experience as the referent; don't use your reading to check your zazen experience. If you do, you will only be disappointed and your zazen will be ruined by the expectations you bring to your cushion from all you have read about what you are supposed to experience. So bring your cushion to your reading, not your reading to the cushion. Read with your body; sit with your mind.

The Ego Is a Sumo Wrestler

Let ego be ego, but sit on it.

SOMEONE ASKED, "WHAT DO I do with my ego? No matter what I do to keep my ego out of my practice, I'm always finding that I'm congratulating myself or beating myself up."

The ego can be a very useful part of your practice. Without it we lose some of the foundation of our practice, one of the tools we have to work with. Don't try to drop the ego directly. Don't try to get rid of it. You can't evict your ego.

The ego is an ass. Like your ass, it's part of the foundation of your zazen practice. However, you don't want to be showing your butt all the time. You don't want to be hearing from it. You don't want it to become your face, and you don't want it to become your voice. But you should let your ego do what it does best, just like your ass. Sit on it.

Just let the ego be the ego, but sit on it. There's no need to stroke it or strike it. It will drop off naturally as your practice continues. The only way the ego wins is if you stop practicing. Then the ego says, "Aha! You can't sit on me. I get to sit on *you!*" And the ego *will* sit on you, all the while getting fatter and heavier, weighing you down with its preferences.

Don't fight the ego. You can't win. The ego is a sumo wrestler. It is much bigger than you and it has a lot of practice pushing you out of center. Just sit on it. Just do zazen. The ego will one day say uncle, but it will do so very quietly. It won't pound the ground or announce it to the world. No referee will be there to raise your hand in victory. The ego will just surrender quietly, hoping you won't notice. Then be very careful because then it becomes dangerous in a new way, a more subtle way. By then, though, if you continue zazen, you will ready for round two.

Doubting Not Doubting

Your practice cannot be whole without doubt.

THERE ALWAYS COMES A TIME in our practice when we are assailed by doubt. Sometimes it comes early and sometimes later. Some of us hold it all the time.

It's very important to know what to do with your doubt, what it consists of, how it works. It's just as important to know what your mind is doing in Zen practice as what your body is doing, how the breath works, how the posture works. Doubt can be tricky.

We often find in the definitions of what a cult is, that a cult will not let you walk away; a cult doesn't allow you to doubt. On the other hand, Zen often actively pushes you away because Zen practice encourages you to doubt, even requires you to doubt, and not just to doubt what you previously believed but to doubt Zen practice itself. Your practice cannot be whole without doubt.

So when you find yourself doubting the efficacy of the practice, of doing zazen; when you find yourself doubting the validity of the teachings, even doubting the sanity of the sangha or the authority of the teacher, that's not necessarily a bad thing. Being without doubt can be much worse because then you become a true believer, a mere follower; you become pious and self-righteous and narrow-minded; you become a real pain in the ass. As Oliver Wendell Holmes said, "I detest a man who knows that he knows." Why? Because, he said, "When you know that you know persecution becomes easy. It is as well that some of us don't know that we know anything."

But when you are in doubt, be sure that you identify exactly what's going on. It's easy to use doubt as a distraction, as an excuse for not practicing. What is practice? Doing what needs to be done. Not practicing, then, is simply not doing what needs to be done. Maybe doing what needs to be done at the time is precisely doubting what needs to be done. But it's very easy to say "sitting is not doing anything, it's not working." Be very careful about using these categorical statements that sound like they exist out there in reality all by themselves as truth. Always ask the question that is begged by such statements: "it's not doing anything—*for whom?*" "It's not working—*for whom?*" Sometimes this is just our ego talking: it's not doing anything—*for me*. It's not working—*for me*. It's too easy to leave out the "for me." Not saying "me" is the rhetorical stealth of the ego.

Doubt is not a bad thing. It allows us to explore more deeply, to put fine points on things, and to find our own way through the practice, our own take on the teachings. We need doubt so that we don't become mere followers along what someone told us was a good path. You can glimpse the way through studying the teachings earnestly, but for your practice to be authentic you have to find your own way through doubt. The greater the doubt the greater the dedication to the practice.

All of us will more or less question the validity of certain teachings: reincarnation, karma, this precept or that. Some experts in Buddhism will say that if you don't believe in this or that doctrine, then you're not a Buddhist. If you don't believe in reincarnation, then you can't be a Buddhist. If you're not a vegetarian—or even a vegan—then you're not a Buddhist. According to their definition you might not be a very *good* Buddhist, but that just shows you a problem with definitions. It's not up to the experts to decide whether you are a Buddhist or not, or even whether you are a good Buddhist or not. Buddhism is bigger than that, more inclusive, more tolerant. It is emptier than that, vast, more spacious. You will hear some teachers and theorists of Buddhism say that you can't pick and choose to decide that this or that doctrine suits you, that you have to take religious belief whole. That's ridiculous. Every sect has already picked and chosen, selected which doctrines it will emphasize and which it will allow to atrophy from lack of belief. But once you have picked and chosen, adhere to your path with courage and determination until doubt assails you again and you have to adjust with even greater courage and determination.

We concentrate on sitting. Sitting allows the weak beliefs that can be killed by the antibiotics of doubt to die off naturally. Zazen helps us to embody what the true teachings are. Whatever teachings you are able to realize on your cushion, that's what Buddhism is right here and now. We are all in development. None of us have "made it," whatever "made it" is supposed to mean.

Doubt is not a bad thing. Just don't be a smart ass about it. Don't ask questions just to be clever. Ask questions that come from your hara, questions that need to be asked, questions that really matter to you. Don't ask questions just to get out of getting up early in the morning. Don't waste your time.

The Korean master Seung Sahn said that it is not enough to "not know." You have to really know not knowing. There is a big difference between just not knowing something and knowing your not-knowing. Just not knowing is ignorance; knowing not-knowing is ego; but not knowing not-knowing is wisdom.

Above all, be sure to doubt your doubt. If you are not doubting your doubt, or doubting your not doubting, it's not true doubt, it's just another kind of conviction. But doubting your doubt does not result in a double negative: it does not cancel itself out and become "faith," although it might lead to a kind of faith, a trust in the practice and your ability to own it. Doubting doubt is like hishiryo consciousness, thinking not thinking. What does Dogen say when asked how to think not thinking? He answers, "not thinking." How do you doubt your doubt? You doubt not doubting. When you doubt your doubt, you get back on the cushion and continue to sit. Just doubting is critical thinking, intelligence; doubting doubt can become merely another kind of faith, not blind faith but clever faith; but by doubting not-doubting we begin to realize the fruits of Zen practice.

A Thorough Knowledge of the Illusion of Self

Precisely that self I haven't thought up is who I really am.
—Kodo Sawaki

I WAS RECENTLY AT A committee meeting where we were discussing the university's student learning outcomes. Someone on the committee objected to one of the outcomes, which said that students "will develop and demonstrate a thorough knowledge of self." Such a goal seemed presumptuous. How would students develop much less demonstrate such a "knowledge"? What would constitute a "thorough" knowledge, and how would we assess it? I jokingly added, "What self? Maybe it would be better to say that students should come out of their university education with a thorough knowledge of the *illusion* of self."

They thought I was joking.

One of the most important things one can get from a university education or from Zen practice is a thorough knowledge of the illusion of self. Nothing could serve us better as we go through our lives than such an understanding, not an intellectual understanding but a really thorough understanding that we embrace with our whole being that indeed our self is a fascinating kaleidoscopic illusion. Everything we are told about who we are, everything we are told about who we are in the world is a fiction, a necessary fiction, as Wallace Stevens said, to help us get us through our lives. We should appreciate that function of self, but we should not mistake it for reality.

No self, muga. No substantial identity, only a constantly shifting, changing portrait of ourselves, a mirror of the reality around us, a faint expression of who we would like to be, who we figure we are, or faintly remember inaccurately as having been. A bundle of necessary fictions. So that when we confront a world that thinks it has a fixed substantial identity or reality, we realize that that's not exactly true. If it were true we would have no influence, no effect on the world as it is. But knowing that it is constantly shifting, we can recreate it, revise it, influence it in small and large ways. To do so, we have to realize that our self is not fixed, not substantial, not set in stone. We are not statues, we are not monuments to ourselves; we are constantly changing, blossoming, breaking down, dissolving, reforming, forming, deforming, unforming, uniforming....

This is what we realize in Zen practice, not who we are, but that we are not. Over and over again. Constantly, endlessly, from birth to death. No self. No *thorough*, no *understanding*, no *knowledge*, no *self*, just living our lives as fully as we can. This is education, true education, this is practice, true practice, true Zen practice. This is what we learn in studying the Dharma, samu, ceremony, posture, breathing, zazen.

On Ceremony

Dust Bowl Dojo

With mushotoku mind the whole world becomes your dojo.

THE PLACE WHERE WE do zazen is called the *dojo*. Dojo means the place where we practice the Way. Some people use it interchangeably with *zendo*, which would mean "Zen way," or alternatively would be an abbreviation of "zazendo," the place where we practice zazen. My master was always adamant that the dojo not be called a zendo. Dojo is the same word used for the place where they practice martial arts. It is a workshop for the heart, a gym for the brain, a studio for the work of the mind, the body-mind. Calling this place the dojo reminds us that Zen is a whole-person discipline not an idea, not a philosophy, not a technique. It is much more than that. Zen practice is nothing less than putting oneself—one's whole self—in harmony with the cosmic order, and the dojo is where we do this together.

Confucius, a long time before Zen existed in its present form, said, "The Way does not glorify the man, the man glorifies the Way." Because this word "glorify" has religious baggage, I would like to substitute "dignify," so we can say, "Zen practice does not dignify the person, the person dignifies Zen practice." It's true. On second thought, maybe glorify is not such a bad description of what happens after all.

A lot of people who come to the dojo expect to be glorified by Zen practice, to be improved by it, to be turned into something extraordinary. In fact, it does improve most people who practice diligently, but that's not the point. If it is the point for you, it won't work. You must keep practicing until it is not the point, and then something extraordinary might happen without your even noticing it. Most people don't stick around long enough to get past the idea that Zen is going to glorify them, that they're going to reach enlightenment, or they're going to have a big breakthrough, a big-bang satori. They are impatient; they think they already grasp the idea of Zen so they walk away with just a taste and none of the sustenance of a strong Zen practice. They don't stick around long enough to realize that the point is not for Zen to glorify them but for them to glorify the Way of Zen.

This is the essence of mushotoku, practicing with no goal. It's very difficult for us in the West. We are always thinking about outcomes, always measuring ourselves, always saying "How am I doing now?" It's as though we never grew up and are always looking for approval from our mother, our father, our teacher, our boss.

Better to think, as my Tai Chi teacher told me, you have already lost the fight; then you have nothing to worry about. Or as Hakuin said, "Young people! Are you afraid of death? Then die now!"

The way is not something that can be measured. It's much more than enlightenment. It's much more than mere mindfulness. There's nothing wrong with mindfulness, but don't mistake mindfulness for the goal. It's not the goal— there is no goal. To mistake mindfulness for the goal is to mistake the finger pointing at the moon for the moon itself. Mindfulness is a byproduct of Zen practice. Enlightenment, too, is a byproduct of Zen practice; it is not the point of Zen practice. Zen practice is itself enlightenment, said Dogen; Zen practice is itself mindfulness—but only if that is not your goal.

Just practice with mushotoku attitude. When we come to the dojo, we just have to practice the Way with no thought of "How am I doing now?" That's all. Concentrate on what we're doing each moment. Concentrate on bowing. Concentrate on posture. Concentrate on breathing. Concentrate on chanting. Concentrate on playing the instruments or on whatever role you're asked to play. Then, gradually, over time, we expand the dojo so that the dojo is not just this room but everywhere you go, and the whole world becomes your dojo. It is the same with samu (work practice): gradually, over time, everything you do becomes samu, and there is no separation between what you do for yourself and what you do for a living and what you do for the Way. It is all Zen practice. Then the Way is not just what we do here in the dojo—our little ceremonies peculiar to our lineage, our quaint etiquettes peculiar to ourselves—but what we do everywhere, respecting each place with its own etiquette peculiar to itself.

Thus we glorify, or dignify, the Way.

Unlike Eiheiji or the New Orleans Zen Temple, our dojo here in Bakersfield happens to be temporary, which shows the changeableness of our lives. We call it the Dust Bowl Dojo, in part to recognize the Dust Bowl migration to this part of California, and in part quoting the Cold Mountain poem about how we humans are like insects skittering in a bowl of dust.

> *We live our lives in a bowl of dust*
> *Like bugs in a clay pot*
> *Circling round and round*
> *Never getting out.*
> *Doomed*

We suffer ceaselessly.
Time flows
And we're old.

Like our lives, this dojo is borrowed space, which shows the interrelatedness of our existences. Our dojo can be broken down and set up in just a few minutes, and yet it is no less a sacred space where we practice the way without leaving a trace, except a whiff of incense. This shows us we can practice anywhere; we don't need an edifice or a church of our own. As much as I sometimes think I might like for us to have such a place, a temple for our practice, I'm thankful we have this moveable dojo and glad we don't have the responsibilities that go with a permanent place of practice. After all, it's not the walls and floors that make a dojo but people together practicing the Way.

What is our practice? It comes in many forms: samu (work practice), ceremony (ritual practice), and above all zazen (sitting practice). Each part of our practice dignifies the Way. We could also say that our practice "certifies" the Way, and the dojo is the workshop where we practice the Way together, where we sometimes take baby steps, sometimes great leaps.

How does our practice work? My master always said, "I don't know how zazen works, but it does." If you want to know how zazen works chemically and biologically, you might read James H. Austin's *Zen and the Brain*, and its sequel *Zen-Brain Reflections*, two huge books (about 1500 pages altogether) published by MIT Press. There you can find out a lot about the thalamus and the hypothalamus, about the chemistry and the electrical system of the brain. But it is much better to just practice. It is the same with work practice and ritual practice—I don't know how they work, but they do. I don't know why we need a dojo, but we do. So come to the dojo and practice earnestly—with mushotoku mind, with no thought of your own profit or gain. The reward is nothing less than putting yourself in harmony with the cosmic order. This is what it means to glorify the Way in the dojo. Where you take the dojo from there is up to you. But remember to take your Zen practice into the world gingerly. Don't rush it. Don't stink of Zen.

Kyosaku!

No spiritual significance.

HERE IN THE DOJO we have many rituals and many instruments, fewer than some dojos and more than others. It can all look very complicated and highly choreographed to the newcomer, but we try to keep it simple. These rituals and instruments do not necessarily have deep significance or meaning, but all of them have a purpose. The *han* calls us to zazen, the gongs announce the beginning and end of zazen, the drum announces the hour, and so on. Administering the kyosaku is another ritual, and the kyosaku itself is another instrument in our orchestra.

The kyosaku is known by many names: the wake-up stick, the pay-attention stick, the encouragement stick, the sword that cuts all delusion. We know it best by what it calls itself: *"WHACK!"*

Many dojos in the U.S. don't know the kyosaku and don't understand its usage. It has been discontinued at many Zen centers as a throwback to the warrior mentality, a quaint artifact of the "macho Zen" of the samurai. They mistake the blow on the shoulders for an act of violence. They mistake the sword that cuts all delusion for a weapon. (I am reminded of a recent case at the University of North Dakota, where a fencing club was forbidden to practice in the gym because sabers and swords were "deemed weapons" and as such were prohibited on campus.) The San Francisco Zen Center stopped using the kyosaku after the Gulf War in

1991 as a gesture in favor of peace. Natalie Goldberg said that after practicing with Dainin Katagiri she never sat in another dojo where it was used. Certainly the stick has been misused—to haze monks in monasteries, to punish monks for minor infractions (*rensaku*), and so on—but these misuses should not be allowed to obscure the day-to-day benefits of its proper use in the dojo. But if the kyosaku's proper use is misunderstood or unappreciated, it's okay not to use it. It's better not to use it at all if it is not understood.

To understand the kyosaku you don't have to grasp its significance or meaning but only its utility, its usefulness as a form of massage. The confluence of acupressure points on the shoulders just near the neck is a center of accumulated tension, where knots of stress can form both before and during zazen. The swift stroke of a well wielded kyosaku can relieve that tension and stress in an instant, breaking it apart and driving it down the body into the floor.

The kyosaku we use in Bakersfield was made by Bob Savage in Alexandria, Louisiana. It is very similar to the one in use at the Alexandria dojo, which bears the same inscription. On both Bob's kyosakus I brushed the calligraphy: "No spiritual significance"—a reminder not to worship or deify the "wake-up" stick even though it sits on the altar and we frame it in ritual. It is essentially another musical instrument, useful and beautiful. Bob handcrafted these kyosakus from cured and aged hard poplar. They are longer and flatter than the oak kyosaku in the New Orleans dojo, which has a hard, stern bite. Bob's kyosakus are sturdy but sleek and well-tuned; their virtue is as much in their bark as their bite. A kyosaku with a strong bite has its greatest effect on the one who receives it. A kyosaku that can also bark benefits everyone in the room.

We can sometimes obsess on the meaning of our rituals and instruments. All of them have a purpose, but that is very different than having a meaning or significance. A purpose implies usefulness, utility. A meaning or significance implies only an abstraction overlaid upon the action. In the dojo we communicate almost exclusively through the instruments. The han calls us to zazen, and near the end of zazen it lets us know that zazen is coming to an end. The large gong accompanies us as we take our places on our zafus. The inkin signals the movements of the godo so that we can follow and not forget where we are in the ceremony. The small gong signals the official start of zazen, the end of zazen and the beginning of kinhin, the end of kinhin, and again the beginning and end of zazen. The big drum signals the hour, and so on.

What does the kyosaku signal?

As those of you who have served as *kyosakuman* know, the kyosaku is framed in *raihai*, the ceremonial bows that show this to be a ritual. After the godo calls "Kyosaku!" the kyosakuman rises and goes to the tatami, bows and walks in gassho to the altar. At the altar he bows and picks up the kyosaku in both hands by holding his palms flat and facing each other with thumbs up, perpendicular to the floor. Holding the kyosaku in this way with arms held straight ahead he bows and returns to the head of the tatami holding the kyosaku in the same way. At the head of the tatami he bows again and then holds the kyosaku with the business end straight up and both hands cupped at the bottom end in front of him. If the godo has not already called "Kyosaku!" then the kyosakuman does so now.

Why all the fanfare? Why all the rigmarole?

This ritual sets the tone of administering the kyosaku. It also sets the tone for receiving the kyosaku. It emphasizes that the kyosaku is not for the gratification of the kyosakuman or his ego. You might be surprised to hear that it is also not only for the relief of the one receiving it. The kyosaku is for the benefit of all existences. If it is not delivered and received in that spirit, it will not have the beneficial effect it is capable of bestowing.

For those sitting in zazen the arrival of the kyosakuman can mean relief from the discomforts of body and mind. There are few distractions to break the unobstructed horizon of zazen, especially when no kusen is spoken to guide the errant mind. The kyosaku provides that break for the body and a chance to move a little, to adjust one's posture before resuming it.

Raising the hands in gassho signals your request to receive the kyosaku. When the kyosaku is felt gently touching the right shoulder, you put your thumbs in your fists, your fists on your knees, and bend your head slightly forward and turning your face slightly away to one side. Ready to receive the "enlightenment" stick, you should remember what is written on the kyosaku—"No spiritual significance"—even as you feel the bite and hear its bark: *"WHACK!"*

The blow should be strong and crisp. It should be neither a thud nor a slap. It should crack like a whip. It should be accurate, landing on the long muscle where the acupressure point gathers stress so that the knot of stress can be broken up and dispersed. Most kyosaku blows, especially by beginners, are too timid, too soft, plunky. Others might be firm and accurate but often lack conviction. They nip rather than bite, or they soothe rather than startle, and their effect wears off before you can finish your bow of acknowledgment. On the other hand, some kyosaku blows can be too harsh and painful, with a sort of afterburn where there should be an afterglow.

I am of course describing as the ideal my master's kyosaku. Sometimes I have felt that his master, Deshimaru, was delivering the kyosaku to my shoulders through him. Everyone else's falls short in some way, including my own. When I sat briefly at the Zen Center of Los Angeles in 2005 while my father was dying, I felt the kyosaku there as a light slap and the sound was like the hollow clap of slit bamboo.

It is often said that one can hear a person's satori in his chanting or how he plays the instruments. It is equally true that one can hear a person's satori in how he delivers the kyosaku. I have noticed too, though, that one's satori can also be heard in the sound their body makes on receiving the kyosaku. The person receiving the kyosaku is a great drum; the kyosaku is the drumstick. The sound that emanates from the shoulders will announce not only the awakening of the kyosakuman, not only the awakening of the person receiving the kyosaku, but also the awakening of everyone in the room. Dogen once had satori when the person next to him received the kyosaku.

To receive the stroke of your master's kyosaku during zazen is a teaching that cannot be duplicated in any other form. It is like receiving his calligraphy and stamp on your rakusu. It is like hearing his voice in dokusan. There is a signature to the stroke of each teacher's kyosaku, as distinctive as a fingerprint or voiceprint.

During his training Deshimaru once responded to a random blow of the kyosaku on top of his head by bounding up, grabbing the kyosaku and beating the kyosakuman with it. This reaction is not to be recommended. He even regretted it himself when his reaction became legendary because everywhere he went, at all the monasteries, the kyosakumen avoided him, and he had to forego the benefits of the stick.

Playing the Instruments in the Dojo

This is true respect, true compassion.

A DAY LIKE TODAY, when the regulars who usually take charge of the dojo and who play the instruments aren't here, is a good time for the rest of us to take up the slack, to learn something, to contribute something. If you've been attentive in your zazen, you will have paid attention to what goes on around you, you will have been sensitive to your surroundings, you will have done more than just sit secluded in your own little universe perched on your zafu. You will have internalized the ceremony, internalized the playing of the instruments, internalized the rhythms of the han, the inkin, the gongs, and the mokugyo. You don't have to have memorized them, that's not necessary because they will have become part of your natural rhythm as you enter the dojo. This makes it much easier to step into the role of shusso, inkin player, mokugyo player, or even the godo, the leader.

We can learn a lot from the various things we do in the dojo whether it is bowing, sampai, sitting, chanting, or playing the instruments. Zazen comes in many forms, after all. When we say that our practice is just sitting, shikantaza, this can be taken as representative of the way we approach a lot of things that we do, especially in the dojo. We often use the word "concentration" to describe the necessary attention that is paid to each of the wholehearted activities to be learned in the dojo. Concentration is a problematic word because people associate it with the mental focus and effort of studying, but Zen concentration is not anything like studying. Maybe a better word would be "absorption." With proper concentration you become absorbed in the action you are performing, no matter how trivial-seeming or momentous. The object of your action becomes an extension of you; you become an extension of the object of your action, like a sponge absorbing water. Properly played, the sound of the mokugyo fills your limbs the way a plant absorbs moisture or nutrients. When you are in tune with your instrument, your body absorbs the tone and vibrations of the gong the way photosynthesis absorbs sunlight.

How is this done? Naturally, spontaneously, without thinking, without memorizing, without mental effort. This doesn't mean that you shouldn't practice, that you don't need discipline to make it work, nor that some amount of intelligence or memorization isn't necessary, especially in the beginning. But it can't be done entirely through mental effort. Study alone won't take you very far. That's why we don't merely memorize the manual on how to do the ceremony, even though we have it written down. We learn by doing with our bodies and minds (or more properly our "body-minds") through trial and error in the dojo, making mistakes, keeping on going.

One of Robert Livingston's early students, Daniel David Feinsmith, who was ordained as a monk and is now a composer in San Francisco, said that when he went that first morning to the dojo in New Orleans and heard the boom of the *taiko* drum near the end of zazen, he marveled at the sound. It was, he said, the most extraordinary and authentic sound he had ever heard, and he had grown up in a musical family. What sort of person could have made that sound? When he found out it was Robert, he decided that Robert would be his teacher so that he could discover the source of that sound. Robert is no musician. But in his hands, the hands of a master, the sound of the drum, the gong, or the kyosaku, is always authentic.

Essentially, all of the instruments are very similar. They must all be played with the same attitude, an attitude of mushotoku. Pride in playing them will spoil your tone. Ego in playing them will cause you to make mistakes. You must not hit them timidly because your fear will spoil the tone. You must not hit them proudly because your pride will spoil the tone. You should hit them with respect and compassion— and confidence. When you hit them hard enough but not too hard, the sound will ring true and clear. I can't describe how it will sound, of course. You know it when you hear it, and you will know it when you hit it. You'll figure out the way to hold the striker for the gong or the mallet for the han so that the sound is clear and solid, not a dull thud or clang or crack, but a clear, candid, appropriate sound.

Each time I start zazen with the three strikes of the small gong it is unique. It doesn't always sound exactly the same. But you will notice that however the first strike sounds, the other two closely resemble the first. To achieve this you need to pay attention, to be absorbed in the action, not in the performance and its result but in the action itself for its own sake. It's not about you, it's not about how well you play, nobody's going to be impressed. There are no Grammy awards for playing the instruments in the dojo.

Take your time. Don't rush through the instrument's role. It's like chanting. Chanting is our first lesson in how to play the other instruments. Our own voice is the primary instrument, the primal instrument, especially the torso where the chant arises from the hara and vibrates through the diaphragm like the shapely and sonorous box of a cello. When we chant the *Hannya Shingyo* we don't rush through it—there are no prizes for getting to the end before everyone else—we chant it together to get the right rhythm and harmony. Once we have internalized the rhythm, memorizing the syllables is easy—even if we don't know what they mean. For any of the instruments to be played correctly, we must understand what they are saying. We don't need to know the meaning of the syllables of the *Hannya Shingyo* but we do need to realize that what they are saying is what they are doing: namely, embodying the complex meaning of the *Heart Sutra*. Meanwhile, the mokugyo keeps time. The han, which often has an inscription that says something like "don't waste time!" calls us to zazen, urging us to practice right here and now. The taiko drum that booms just before the end of zazen marks the hour of day and wakes you up if you're drowsing. The small and large gongs have the job of announcing the beginnings and endings of zazen and kinhin, as well as providing ceremonial marks of punctuation and emphasis. More complicated is the meaning of the inkin, which seems to be conducting (or protecting) the godo, but is actually being conducted by the godo, who in this way instructs the assembly with his body, through movement and sound, on what to do during the ceremony.

People usually start learning the instruments by playing the han and the mokugyo. The three simple accelerations of the han, that block of wood that calls us to zazen, give us time to transition from the world into the dojo. Don't rush it. Let the discrete strikes breathe, all the way to the end. Find the sweet spot on the wood that produces the right tone. It should not sound hard like a crack, nor soft like a tap. It should have a voice of authority, neither strident nor arrogant, neither timid nor reticent, but clear and confident. This includes the final coda after the three accelerations, which consists of two additional strikes and a third "thunk" on the side or edge of the han.

Like the han with its simple accelerations, the mokugyo lets you concentrate on an unchanging melody, setting the tempo of chanting the *Hannya Shingyo*. A blind person can play the mokugyo because you don't have to follow what everyone else is doing; everyone else has to follow you—for better or worse. The rhythm should be regular, even monotonous, at least as it is played in our lineage's dojos, a strike for each syllable or each set of syllables in the *Hannya Shingyo*. (For an extended discussion and analysis of the *Hannya Shingyo*, see my edition of Deshimaru's commentaries on the sutra, *Mushotoku Mind: The Heart of the Heart Sutra*. Hohm Press, 2012.) Establishing this rhythm is fairly easy when we chant the sutra just once, but during the longer ceremony, when we chant it three times, it gets a little harder because the mokugyo player has to increase the tempo the second time around, and then increase it even more with the third repetition, then reining in this tempo and winding it down in the final notes before coming to a full stop.

After getting comfortable with playing the mokugyo, you can move on to the inkin. The inkin is very different than the mokugyo because instead of leading the chant, you are being led by the movements of the godo. In effect, the godo is playing the inkin with his body. On the approach to the dojo, he rings the inkin with his walk, allowing one ring for every several steps. As he stops and steps into the dojo, he must pause and step, spacing the rings according to the rhythm that has been established by his approach. Bowing during sampai, he plays it with his waist, and with his head as it rises from the mat. So the inkin player is obliged to pay close attention to the movements of the godo and be sure that the ringing of the bell is synchronized with these movements. A good way to practice playing the inkin is to play godo, going through the leader's motions with your own body, approaching the dojo, stepping into the dojo, bowing after entering the dojo, bowing to the shusso, stepping up to the altar, offering incense, coming around the mat and laying out the *zagu*, knowing with your body that the last strike of the inkin coincides with the dropping of the edges of the zagu on the mat, and so on through sampai.

The instrument that most of us learn to play last is the gong, usually played by the shusso, the head monk or assistant to the godo. A common error in playing the gong is to strike it on top or on the body of the metal instead of at a forty-five degree angle on the edge. Another common error is to strike it too hard. One might assume that the powerful sound of the gong comes from a powerful hand, but actually the power in the sound comes from the inner power of a steady hand. You need not strike the gong any harder than you would tap the back of a child to get its attention. Then, spacing the strokes, especially at the beginning of an acceleration, get a good feeling for the clarity of the sound. Don't rush it. The acceleration should cut the timing of the strokes almost in half, each time you hit it, a little faster each time, but not so fast that you can't distinguish the final strikes. The last strikes should remain as clear and distinct as all the others, all the way to the end of the acceleration. Then, after the last strike in the acceleration, let the vibration of the gong almost die out before you put the period on the acceleration with the pause and then the final strike, which should sound as clear as the first one that began the series.

There is one more instrument that we don't always think of as an instrument, but it too is part of the ceremony and we should treat it very much as we treat any other instrument, play it as we play any other instrument. That is the kysosaku. We should treat the kyosaku with the same care that we treat the other instruments, with the absorption of mushotoku. With the strike of the kyosaku on the shoulders, the shusso plays your body like an instrument so that you can feel the vibrations that the gong or the mokugyo feels, so that you can resound to the cosmos and identify with the instruments that you play in the ceremony. The kyosaku is the final instrument we learn to play.

What makes playing the instruments difficult is if we get too concerned with what we're doing. We sometimes think that concentrating and being in the moment here and now is focusing very hard on what we are doing. But being too concerned with what we are doing (that is, worrying too much whether we are doing it right or wrong) is not true concentration, not true attention to your environment, not true absorption in your action. The problem arises only if you have not been paying attention until now, when you are called upon to act. Remember the word "play" in "playing" the instruments, and don't take yourself too seriously.

You should always be aware of everything that's going on around you. Someday the other instrument players won't be here and you'll need to step up. Someday I won't be here and someone will need to step up. Same thing in life. In everyday life, at home, in your job, one day everything changes, someone doesn't show up and it's up to you to take on the responsibility. Are you ready? You have your routine down to a system, everything is going smoothly, and then something happens, something changes, and you have to adjust. You step up. The reason we don't change the ceremony or the dojo etiquette is so that we can recognize the small changes when they occur, and they always occur. Even when everything looks the same it's different. We need to appreciate those differences.

Playing the instruments is not just some ancient ritual that we perpetuate because it provides some sort of superstitious spiritual comfort; there is no magic in ceremony, no invocation to a higher power. It's just part of the practice, part of the discipline. It's the way we humble ourselves, not before tradition or religion but before these instruments, before the altar, not because there's a Buddha on the altar or because we think we're Buddhists, but because the altar is there, because the flowers are there, because the kyosaku is there. All of these things we need to take care of just as we need to take care of all beings in our realm of influence. These are some of the beings, however numerous, that we vow to take care of as one of the four bodhisattva vows. These are some of the "all existences" that we are paying respect to when we put our hands together in gassho.

So don't get caught up in your own small and self-centered ideas of what ceremony is, what playing the instruments means, and most of all what the significance of what all these things is. Don't worry about what concentration is or what absorption is because these are just words pointing at the right attitude which, like the sound of a well-struck gong, you will know when you hear it. Just let yourself relate to the things around you so that you can take care of them in these simple ways, and they'll take care of you. This is true respect, true compassion.

Empty Ceremony

Ceremony is not different than everyday life.

PEOPLE ALWAYS WANT TO know about the ceremony: what does it mean? But the ceremony, our ceremony, is meaningless. It is empty. This is very important. The ceremony is empty of significance so that the whole universe can flow into it. The ceremony includes nothing and excludes nothing, and therefore everything fills emptiness. *Form becomes emptiness; emptiness becomes form. Form is exactly emptiness; emptiness is exactly form.* This is the thesis of the *Heart Sutra* which we chant every day. It is the verbal reflection of zazen, and it is the verbal embodiment of our ceremony, the opening and closing of the body in sampai, the expansion and contraction of our bodies in breathing, the coming and going of pain in our knees and back. All of this is the reflection or embodiment of one thing: zazen. Ceremony is not different than everyday life. When we ask, "What is the significance of ceremony?" we would do better to ask, "What is the significance of our everyday life?" Why do we perform these empty rituals? When ceremony and everyday living become one continuity of motion and stillness, emptiness and form, then we have answered the only question that is worth asking, the only question that is worth developing a practice for, a discipline for.

To Bow or Not to Bow to Buddhas

Recognizing your fundamental nature.

A CHINESE POET WROTE: "I don't bow to Buddhas." This seeming irreverence puzzled me for a long time. Why not bow to Buddhas? Who doesn't bow to whom? Do Buddhas bow to me? When I bow, what do I bow to? If everything has Buddha nature, how can I not bow to Buddhas? Does a dog have Buddha nature?

In Zen practice we don't make that separation, that distinction between what bows and what is bowed to. When you bow, it should be a complete action, no separation between who bows and what is bowed to. Just like sitting. When you're sitting you should be just sitting, no separation between you and your environment. And if you're just sitting, you'll be doing exactly what the Buddha did—recognizing your fundamental nature. That's what we bow to, not to Buddhas, but we are Buddhas bowing to Buddhas. Or rather—and this is as precise as I can be—we are simply Buddhas bowing. The zazen posture, like the rest of Zen practice, looks modest, but it's really very powerful. Not proud, but strong. Not weak, not soft, not submissive, but supple, flexible, willing to bend.

This is why we bow.

Because It Is Empty

*We should be always moving away from mythological beliefs
and toward a simplification of our practice.*

BECAUSE IT IS EMPTY, Zen always takes on the values
of the culture where it finds itself, absorbs those values and
transforms them. Sometimes Zen allows for distortions of
that culture, and when it does it eventually drops them.
In China, Chan added its Taoist and Confucian rules of
obedience and order. In Japan, Zen added Shinto reverence
for the ancestors and political leaders. The patriarchal,
misogynistic, militaristic, and nationalist additions were not
always happy. Many of these accidental, cultural trappings
we should let drop away. When some practice or belief does
not work here and now, we should let it die a natural death.
Trappings are traps.

In America many of these trappings persist, and some
in the American (and European) Zen priesthood stray
farther from the basis of Zen practice and adopt more of
the exotic trappings: *oriyoki* bowls, Dharma names, sutra
chanting, honoring obscure bodhisattvas with provincial
and parochial origins, like Jizo, which appeals to Japanese
ancestor worship and its "protection" of children and the
dead. It is worthwhile asking why an American priesthood
would want to perpetuate the worship of this figure. Maybe
Jizo fills a gap in our mythology, since we have no protector
devoted to caring for children and the dead. Still, we should
be always moving away from mythological beliefs and

toward a simplification of our practice, always paring down the inessential in our practice, not adding to these adopted beliefs, merely trading in Jesus for Jizo.

This is one of the big questions for Zen in America, discovering what is necessary, what is essential or integral to the practice and what is incidental. This is a delicate operation, though, because we must be careful not to throw out the baby with the baby protectors.

People may be confused about the relationship of zazen with Zen, Buddhism, Taoism, Christianity, and other religions, but it's really very simple. Culturally, intellectually, philosophically, historically, it can become very complex. But essentially, Zen—or rather zazen—is at the root of the religious impulse. It transcends religious doctrine, religious dogma, religious history, and specific religious icons. As Lao-tzu said, what can be said about the Way is not the Way. Anything that can be said about Zen in relation to Buddhism, Taoism and so on—and much can be and has been said about their philosophical and historical connections—is not essentially relevant to the practice and experience of zazen. These are all interesting contexts in which to place the practice, culturally, religiously, historically, intellectually, philosophically. But we shouldn't confuse these contexts with zazen itself. These contexts have changed over time and will continue to change. The experience of zazen doesn't change.

When we talk about the Three Treasures of Zen—Buddha, Dharma, and Sangha—there are complicated ways to talk about them and there are simple ways. Simply, Buddha means zazen; Dharma means the teaching and the reality it expresses; and Sangha means the other people with whom we practice, extending to all other existences.

In a Taoist context, zazen is the still meditation Chi Kung, a complement to the moving meditation of Tai Chi. In a Buddhist context we extinguish ego; in a Taoist context we generate *chi (ki)* through the art of sitting and forgetting. One can practice zazen in a Christian context, a Muslim context, and so on. The context is not important; only the center of the practice is important, which is the emptiness at the center of the context of your choice. The context is like the place of practice, which might be a room, a mountaintop, a precipice, or the middle of a highway. The center of the practice is still the emptiness of zazen. And zazen fills the emptiness of Zen.

Mondo and Dokusan

The authentic koans always come from our own lives.

IMMEDIATELY FOLLOWING ZAZEN, immediately following ceremony, we have mondo. This is a time to ask the questions you have about Zen practice. Unlike a kusen, when the teacher gives instruction during zazen, and unlike a Dharma talk, teisho, which is more like a lecture, mondo allows for an authentic and spontaneous exchange, face-to-face and mind-to-mind, about our immediate concerns here and now.

Fresh from zazen, refreshed as though we have just woken up from a nap, we can allow these questions to arise naturally and we can take in the answers naturally. Many koans come from famous exchanges, mondo, that were in some way representative, evocative, useful. They become "cases" that were passed down and anthologized to be studied because they set precedents, just like in law. "Case" is what koan means. There are, as you know, two kinds of law. Civil law is legislated and codified so that it works through prohibition and anything that is not explicitly against the law is okay. That is the kind of law they have on the European continent and in Louisiana. Case law, though, also called "common law," is based on precedent, on cases that have been settled by the courts previously. This is the kind of law that is practiced in England and in the other forty-nine states. Koans, we might say, are precedents that remain unsettled, or cases that must be settled again and again by each Zen student.

We might say that there are two ways to practice religion, too, through rules and regulations or through the exemplary experience of cases. In Buddhism, in Zen, these kinds of practice can be seen, too. A practice based on rules and regulations interprets the precepts very narrowly, legalistically, literally, and relies heavily on the sutras and other texts. This kind of practice is not true Zen practice. We don't bother much with the letter of the precepts, which have been reduced over time to the ten *kai* that we affirm when we are ordained, which are summarized in the Three Pure Precepts ("to cut all evil, to practice the good, to help all beings"), which are in turn distilled into the single precept of zazen, the highest precept, encompassing and embodying all the others. All the other precepts are just micromanaging.

Koan practice can be undertaken as a curriculum through which one passes, as it is in Rinzai, or it can be the study of precedents, as in Soto. In Soto Zen, we sit and let koans pass through us. Koans are our supplemental reading list, our literary heritage, our mythology. In Rinzai, you are given a koan by the master and you sit with it for weeks, months, or years until you can grasp it not with your intellect but with your entire being. We deal with koans, too: zazen itself is our first koan, the first Dharma gate through which we must pass. We confront other koans, but they are not from the texts, *The Gateless Gate* or *The Blue Cliff Record*. Those are the study guides for the big questions. The authentic koans always come from our own lives.

In addition to mondo, where we have a group discussion about our questions, we also have dokusan. Dokusan in Rinzai is the private interview in which master and student explore the koan curriculum in one-on-one intimacy.

It is regular and frequent, although each meeting might last only a minute or two. In our lineage we have dokusan but much more sparingly because we have no koan curriculum. You might have a question, a life koan that is too intimate to be discussed with the group. You might have life koans that you don't even want to discuss with me. That's fine. Sit with it. Sit with it as you sit with your zazen koan, with musho-toku mind, until the case is settled. But know that dokusan is available to you, as is mondo, for your questions. Dokusan might also be initiated by your teacher to discuss important issues of practice. Mondo and dokusan, two forms of practice that you can take advantage of.

Question: *What about the koan about the Bull that entered through the door with head and body but couldn't get its tail through. It seems like it's a metaphor for something.*

It's a metaphor, that's true. But koans always resist the intellectualization and interpretation that is available through mere literary analysis and analogy. A really good metaphor, though, is like the Bull: while most of its meaning can get through the gate of interpretation, there will always be a part that can't get through. That is the part that we are aware resists interpretation, resists totalization of meaning. For me, this is a profound koan because it resonates with my experience of becoming a Zen teacher.

I had gone through the ceremony of authorization, but there was a part of me (my tail, or my ass) that I was aware did not fit through the Dharma gate. It was only a small part of me, perhaps, even the least part of me as a teacher, but it kept me from passing through. The shusso ceremony acknowledges this feeling of inadequacy with a sincere profession of one's unworthiness. And yet my master has said that I can do some good after all. This mondo between Docho Roshi and the Shusso reflects the non-symbolic nature of the teaching practice. "What can you do with this *shippei*?" "I can use it for life, and I can use it for death." This is the actual severity of the teaching, the power of the teacher, and it is an awesome responsibility before which the new teacher may hold his head and body erect and immoveable, but at which his tail trembles.

On Ordination

Understanding Ordination

Ordination is very simply an expression of your serious intention to practice zazen.

ORDINATION. LAY ORDINATION. Bodhisattva ordination. What does it mean?

Bodhisattva ordination is the first bow you take in the dojo, the first breath during zazen, the first step during kinhin, clearing your throat as you begin the first syllable of the chant, the *Hannya Shingyo*, the first spoonful of genmai in the morning.

Ordination is not a contract; it has nothing to do with the future. If you take the vows as pertaining to the future, you misunderstand them. Ordination is here and now. Taking the precepts is always here and now. Each moment is eternally renewed in your vows. The rakusu worn today is a renewal of your vows. There is no other way.

Most of us would like to understand ordination before we make the step, before we make the leap of faith. But I'm sorry to say that you can't understand ordination beforehand. You have to trust the impulse to be ordained; it is like falling in love with the person you are going to spend the rest of your life with. You don't have to understand; you just know. I didn't understand beforehand what it meant to be ordained. Being ordained without fully understanding what it means to be ordained is the very heart of being ordained: a leap of faith.

Ordination does not make you a different person, a better person. It doesn't make you a more pious person (god forbid).

After ordination you are just as much a buddha as you were before. You do, though, see this sameness in a different light, a better light. Ordination is like opening your eyes in bed after you have lain awake for some time. It's like turning off the reading lamp after the sun has come up.

For those of you who have taken bodhisattva ordination, for those of you who are planning to take ordination, and for those of you who are not interested in ordination at all, I want to say a few words about bodhisattva or lay ordination, especially the ordination ceremony itself. There are four parts to the ceremony: taking refuge, home-leaving, taking the precepts through "formless repentance," and receiving the rakusu and a Dharma name. You don't necessarily need to understand these parts of the ceremony to take ordination, but you might want to have an idea of what it's all about.

1. Taking Refuge in the Three Treasures

Now we take refuge in the Three Treasures of Buddha, Dharma, and Sangha. The Buddha is our zazen, the Dharma is the teachings we practice, and the Sangha is all the Beings we practice with. Taking refuge in the Three Treasures means throwing ourselves into them without hesitation, trusting in them completely.

The first part is taking refuge in the Three Treasures: the Buddha (zazen), the Dharma (the teachings), and the Sangha (practice with and for others). This is comparatively straightforward. If you don't have some idea of the Three Treasures, you have not yet begun to practice and shouldn't be taking ordination.

2. Home-Leaving

As we leave home, we pay our respects to our families, bowing
towards our birthplace. For the bodhisattva this represents
honoring the lay life that is the field of our practice.

In the home-leaving ceremony you bow to the place of your
birth in a gesture of respect and symbolic abandonment
of your life to this point. Like other parts of the ceremony,
home-leaving is not to be taken literally, especially as lay
practitioners. Home-leaving doesn't mean that you leave
your parents or your family behind, and still less your spouse
or your children. It is a momentary abandonment, a dropping off, a shedding of attachment. It is all right to be attached to your family, it's natural—but it is also natural not
to become so attached to your family that it becomes a liability for them and for you.

Home-leaving is like the story of the young monk who
went up the mountain to find enlightenment. When he met
an older monk coming down the mountain, he asked him if
he had found what he was looking for up there. The older
monk nodded. What was it like? The older monk let the bundle he was carrying drop to the ground. What would he do
now? The older monk picked up the bundle and continued
down the mountain, returning to the world.

Bowing to the place of your birth, you say goodbye to the
person you have been until now, dropping the bundle of that
identity, the burden of self, only to pick it all up again and
continue on, going back to your family, your job, and your life
with renewed purpose. Receiving the rakusu and a Dharma
name at the end of the ordination ceremony commemorates

the nature of that vow of renewed purpose and your seriousness in following through with it.

3. Taking the Precepts through Formless Repentance

Unlike formless repentance, the ten precepts (kai) are relatively easy to understand. Not killing, not stealing, not abusing sex, not abusing alcohol, and so on. It doesn't mean you won't drink alcohol, or have sex, or kill plants or animals, but your relationship to these actions will change. Rather than a literal or legalistic conception of the precepts, you need to develop a relationship with the precepts that allows them to take root naturally, automatically, spontaneously through the practice of zazen. All the precepts are contained in zazen.

If you do zazen, you will listen to what your body and your mind—your body-mind—have to tell you, and you will come closer to adhering to the precepts naturally. You might eat too much red meat and discover during zazen that your joints ache. You might have drunk too much red wine last night and find that you're a little hungover this morning. You might smoke and find that you don't breathe so well. In this way zazen teaches us to back off and moderate our activities along the lines of the precepts. It is the same for the mind as for the body. During zazen, things you have done in the past might arise in your mind, you might feel regret, they might haunt you and trouble your conscience, just as the red meat and red wine come back to haunt your organs. A kind of repentance might result from this reflection: you might discover that you'd like to say you're sorry to someone as a natural result of sitting zazen.

This brings us to formless repentance, also known as confession, probably the most difficult part of the ceremony to understand. The *Confession Sutra*, chanted before receiving the precepts, is a form of repentance:

All my past mistakes and misdeeds
Which were the result of greed, anger and ignorance
From now on, I vow in front of everyone
That my body, mind and words follow the true perfect Way.

All sorts of things arise during zazen as a result of karma. The aching joints that come from eating too much red meat are due to karma; the slight headache from drinking too much red wine, karma; regrets too are karma. Katagiri talks about "the ocean of karmic hindrances that emerge from delusion." He says of them, "If you want to repent of these delusions, you must sit in zazen." To understand these statements, we need to know what we mean by "karma," what "hindrances" are, and what "delusion" is.

Karma is simply cause and effect, action and its consequences. For this reason, as you have heard me say before, there is no good karma and no bad karma, there is just karma. Distinguishing between good and bad karma is just our ego's interpretation imposed upon the "suchness" of the way-things-are-as-they-are. The way things are can be called "bad" only because it *appears*—in a limited context—to affect us in a way that is personally inconvenient or causes us or those we care about pain; the way things are is "good" only because it appears to affect us in a happy, beneficial, or profitable way. Quite apart from the fact that appearances can be deceiving, the act of interpretation itself is a "hindrance" to seeing the "suchness" of existence, the way-things-are-as-they-are. These hindrances come in negative and positive forms, but they all wrap us in delusion when we try to interpret karma as good or bad.

As we know from the *Shinjinmei*, the act of choosing itself is what involves us in an endless cycle of discrimination. This is our original *bonno*, the origin of all our delusions, our "issues." There may be an analogy in Christian mythology's original sin.

In the Garden of Eden, when Adam and Eve ate from the Tree of the Knowledge of Good and Evil, they began their cycle of suffering, which was due to interpreting the phenomena in the Garden dualistically: good/evil, male/female, pure/impure, man/beast, human/divine, natural/unnatural, naked/clothed, and so on. This was an original loss of the sense of the unity (interdependence) of all existences. They continued to suffer because they were not allowed to eat from the other forbidden tree in the garden, the Tree of Eternal Life, which would have reversed the estrangement of so-called opposites.

This forbidden tree, the Tree of Eternal Life, unavailable once the fruit of the tree of discrimination is tasted, is the Bodhi Tree, the tree of enlightenment, the tree of nirvana, the very tree that the Buddha sat under, the one that returns us to the original state before the fall into the this-instead-of-that of choosing, of discriminating, of desire, and of suffering. Zazen returns us to this state of nondiscrimination, beyond good and evil, before good and evil, so that we can return to this world, here and now, to deal with good and evil with an enlightened perspective, one that is not dominated by the ego and its selfish interpretations. This is the mushotoku attitude of being-in-time which is zazen.

The ego is like a teenage boy with raging hormones, like an empty belly that knows only its own hunger. It is a bottomless pit of sexual desire, of insatiable appetite. You can feed and feed the desire and never reach the end of appetite. It is the same with the ego and its curiosity that investigates, discriminates, interprets, and judges. It is a bottomless pit of judgment built upon interpretation, interpretation built upon discrimination, discrimination built upon fact, fact selected by assertions of desire, desire built upon nothing at all except its own emptiness. This is the truth to be found by going deeply into our own delusion. This is why we say that delusion is itself satori.

The other day on NPR (National Public Radio) there was a report on a great sinkhole in Florida. It came out that sinkholes are not isolated incidents; they are more common than we think. The interviewer seemed appalled that these sinkholes cannot be predicted or measured in advance, that insurance companies cannot calculate their actuarial occurrence and so are at a loss about how to charge premiums for them. If a great sinkhole swallows a house or a neighborhood, how do we combat it?

The sinkhole is a rich metaphor. The threat of the sinkhole collapsing under our feet at any moment is mujo: the constant change that comes without warning and that can strike anyone, anywhere, at any time, in any number of forms, as a sinkhole, a hurricane, an earthquake, or disease. The revenge of a sinkhole is a vivid illustration of karma. Actions taken by companies extracting brine or water or oil from the earth eventually have geological consequences, karmic consequences. Buddhists who take reincarnation literally and karmic consequences as cosmic justice might say that people's houses had fallen into one of these sinkholes as a result of a past lifetime of ill-doing, bad karma, and so justice had been done, just desserts. Even if we can find no source in the person's present lifetime, this line of thought sees the sinkhole as payback for some ill done in a previous lifetime. I hope it is clear that this is nonsense and superstition and not just silly nonsense but pernicious nonsense that blames the victim, no better than Pat Robertson blaming Hurricane Katrina on the bad behavior of the city of New Orleans.

Karmic hindrances, then, come in many forms, one of which is the temptation to interpret cause and effect according to our own limited point of view and self-interest. These are delusions, like any other, and we must work to get past them. One way to do this is to "repent" of them.

There are really two kinds of repentance: what I might call "ethical repentance" and "ontological repentance." Ethical repentance is individual repentance: we regret a specific action and say we're sorry. Ontological repentance, or "formless repentance," is more general. Shohaku Okamura, one of Kosho Uchiyama's disciples, distinguishes between the two kinds of repentance very succinctly when he says: "In this [latter] kind of repentance we do not actually say something like, 'I'm sorry because of this or that specific mistake,' Rather, our zazen is itself repentance" (*Living by Vow*, 58). Ontological repentance is mushotoku repentance, repentance with no object and no expectation of forgiveness in return for that repentance.

When we bow, we bow to no object but to the ocean of karmic delusion. When we sit down in zazen, we gassho and bow once to the zafu and once to the center of the dojo. The first bow is a specific gesture of respect to the existence that props us up, the zafu. The second bow is a gesture of respect for all existences. Two kinds of bow, just like the two kinds of repentance. We don't bow to any object or with any object in mind. We don't bow to buddhas. We do samu, work practice, in the same spirit. Sweeping the floor or cleaning toilets has no intrinsic value. When we chant the *Heart Sutra*, it is in the same vein with mushotoku spirit, the attitude of formless repentance—not to save your own soul, or anyone else's, but to drown the ego in the ocean of karmic hindrances.

In fact, we frame our zazen with raihai—the ceremony of gassho, bowing, sampai—before and after zazen, as an instance of formless repentance. When the kyosakuman bows before and after striking you on the shoulders, it frames his formless repentance. In this way we prepare to sit in zazen, where we drown the ego and its interpretations in the ocean of karmic hindrances and delusions. When we sit in zazen we sit at the edge of the abyss, looking into the sinkhole of ego. We sit by the edge of the ocean of karmic hindrances and delusions and observe their vastness, their insatiable nature. This is why in the Four Great Bodhisattva Vows that we chant every day, we acknowledge that existences are numberless, yet we vow to take care of them all; bonno are endless, yet we vow to end them all; Dharma gates are innumerable, yet we vow to pass through them all; and the Buddha Way is unknowable, yet we vow to follow through.

This is why Dogen calls zazen itself enlightenment-practice. Not because it will get you to a better place or make you a better person but because looking into the sinkhole of delusion is enlightenment itself. Ordination is very simply an expression of your serious intention to practice enlightenment-practice through zazen.

4. Receiving the Rakusu and a Dharma Name

Receiving the rakusu and a Dharma name is the climax of the ordination ceremony. Whether we have sewn our own rakusu or had it sewn for us, the rakusu is a great treasure. In the past the rakusu was sewn out of worthless, discarded cloth and dyed to a hue indistinguishable from earth to symbolize its worthlessness. Yet the care with which it is cut and stitched, and the care with which it is inscribed with the names of teacher and student, invest it with a significance and power that is priceless. No bodhisattva treats his or her rakusu cavalierly. Many new bodhisattvas want to wear the rakusu all the time. Some wear it over their clothes; some wear it inside their clothes. It is only necessary, though, to wear it during zazen and, if you like, during samu.

Finally, you receive the rakusu, kneeling in front of your teacher, who passes it through the billowing smoke of the incense, and take it like a bird in your hands. At that moment, making eye contact with your teacher, you hear your Dharma name spoken for the first time. It has an exotic ring to it, not only in Japanese but also its meaning in English. "You are Reishin," I heard my master say, "Profound Mind," or, years later, during the monastic ordination ceremony, "You are Taisen, Great Abandonment." Your master has given you this name in part as a reflection of your character and in part as an encouragement of your potential, something to live up to. Having received this name, you will never be the same.

Sewing the Field of the Kesa

To sew your kesa is to sow the field of your practice.

AFTER ZAZEN SOMEONE REMARKED, "When I felt most attuned and at peace was when you all were chanting near the end of zazen."

There is good reason for this response. What she heard was the *Kesa Sutra* chanted at the end of zazen by those who have taken the precepts and been ordained as monks or lay practitioners. The *Kesa Sutra* is the expression of the field of practice. It says that we wrap ourselves in the kesa (or rakusu) as we wrap ourselves in the practice of helping all beings. The design of the kesa or rakusu, the "formless robe of great freedom," is a rice field that stands for the fruitfulness of our practice. It is an orderly design, like the practice, orderly in space and time.

The kesa or rakusu is *sewn* just as a field is *sown*. These two words are related linguistically in the Middle English word *sowen*. More interesting still is that these words are of Indo-European origin with a connection to *suture*, which is related to the word *sutra*, a stitching or sewing together.

As you sew the kesa, you sow the seeds of your practice. We chant the *Kesa Sutra* about the rakusu that is sutured on the model of a field that is sown through practice.

Dai sai geda puku	*O Formless Robe of great freedom*
Muso fuku den e	*The field of practice beyond form and emptiness.*
Hibu nyorai kyo	*Wearing the Buddha's teaching*
Kodo sho shujo.	*I vow to help all beings.*

To sew your kesa is to sow the field of your practice. We all sew our kesas in different ways, not always by joining cloth together, just as there are many ways to sow the field of our practice, to fulfill the vows of the precepts. Again, zazen is the foremost way to fulfill the precepts, which is why we chant the *Kesa Sutra* at the end of zazen.

Today We Have Ordination

(New Orleans Zen Temple, 19 July 2014)

TODAY WE HAVE BODHISATTVA ordination. Like zazen, each person's ordination looks very similar to people on the outside. But as you know, every zazen is unique to you every time you sit down. Like zazen, the power of the vows in your ordination cannot be conferred on you by anyone. This is just the outer ritual to formalize and symbolize what you have already done inside. Our zazen is not *tariki* (other power) but *jiriki* (self power). Just as with zazen and Zen in general, the significance is what you make of it, in your practice, your daily practice.

Some parts of the ceremony will resonate more for some of you than others. For some it will be taking refuge in the Three Treasures. For some it will be one or more of the kai, the vows. For others it will be Daichi Zenji's powerful and poetic "Dedication to the Samurai." For still others it will be the explanation of the *kesa*. Whatever it is that resonates with you, you will take that with you wherever you go from now on.

Just remember that in taking ordination you are not joining a particular sangha, a particular temple; you are entering a lineage, a stream of those who have gone before and those who will follow. It's good to be a member of the temple, but that membership is very different than receiving ordination, which involves you in a much larger community. Wherever you go you will always be connected to that lineage, part of the greater sangha that enjoys the support of the kesa.

For me bodhisattva ordination was transformative. It changed my life. Like putting a gyroscope on an out-of-control rocket. Monastic ordination, not so much. At the time, I compared my bodhisattva ordination to staying up all night reading by lamplight, only to realize that the sun had come up. For me, ordination was simply a matter of switching off the artificial, intellectual light and seeing instead with the full, natural light of wisdom practice. It shattered me. It was a personal breakthrough, an opening inward to the world, just as becoming a Zen teacher much later on was an opening outward to the world. That was just my experience; you will have your own.

As Robert says, Zen is a do-it-yourself operation. But the sangha is here, as you know, to support you in your practice. You may not even realize how important a support this sangha is, and can be, even if you live far away, even for those members of the extended sangha who have never been here. Little by little, the practice spreads. And the spreading of the practice happens only through you—not through your proselytizing but through your concentration, your zazen.

Timshel: Taking the Precepts Means Taking Responsibility

Thou mayest!

THIS MORNING READING STEINBECK'S East of Eden, I finished the chapter about the title, right in the center, right at the heart of the book. As you may know, the title comes from the story of Cain and Abel in the Bible. It is a story about what one brother does to another because of the disfavor that one of them finds in the eyes of God, or, in the parallel stories in the novel, in the eyes of the father. Two sons compete for the love of the father, and because one feels less favored a lot of suffering follows.

The Chinese cook, Lee, has an interesting perspective on this Biblical story, which resonates with him. He feels the story of Cain and Abel is the story of all humanity. So he takes it to the Chinese elders of the Lee clan in San Francisco. These sages get so interested in the story that they bring in a couple of rabbis because they want to find out what the original story said. They feel that the interpretation of the story hinges on one word, *timshel*, in Hebrew. They see that in the King James Version it is translated as *"Thou shalt."* In the American Standard Version it is translated as *"Doest thou."* They see a difference between those two because *Thou shalt* seems to be a promise or a prophecy. *Thou shalt* suffer or *thou shalt* experience this or that determined fate because of what happened between the two brothers.

But *"Doest thou"* is an order, a command. That seems to mean that you *will* suffer, that you should suffer, that you should or should not do this or that, not as a determined fate but as a judgment. So between the promise or the prophecy and the divine order, they see a big difference and they want to find out what the real, original intent was in the authoritative Hebrew text. So after spending several years in consultation with rabbis, scholars, and each other, they discover that there is a third meaning, a third way of taking that word *timshel*. And that is, *"Thou mayest."* So then the outcome becomes a choice. It becomes something that one may or may not do. Thou mayest find that you sin and suffer. They feel that this is the original intent, but also that whether one chooses to hear that word in the first, second, or third translation determines who you are, what kind of person you are, and what your fate will be. The Greeks believed that character is destiny; these Chinese elders believe that interpretation is destiny.

I bring up this story because it seems to me to be a good way to understand how we take the Buddhist precepts, the kai. In the translation that we used when I took the precepts and when you took the precepts it was "Do not kill," "Do not steal," and so on. But that has always seemed not quite right to me, close to accurate, but it never sat well. It all sounded a little too much like the Ten Commandments, like we were taking orders rather than taking responsibility—because the precepts are much more of a choice, not a prophecy and not a command. The value of taking the precepts and practicing zazen comes from the confrontation with the possibility that you can act in any number of ways, being free, that you can choose to follow the precepts or not. It is the choosing that determines your practice, not the mouthing of the words in a ceremony, not a more or less vague or sincere vow taken at a moment in time.

It is much more in the spirit of Zen to say, "Thou mayest steal," or in the case of taking the precepts, "I may steal." It doesn't mean you have permission to steal but that you are always subject to the same potential actions that any other human being might do under the right or wrong circumstances.

If the Cain and Abel story really is a fundamental story of humanity, it seems that this is an important story to interpret correctly from whatever religious perspective: Hebrew scholar, Confucian sage, Taoist immortal, Zen bodhisattva. It becomes a fundamental story for Zen practice as well, since Zen is about the fundamental realities. From the outside, taking the precepts may look to some people like taking orders from on high. On the contrary, taking the precepts is not taking orders; taking the precepts is taking responsibility.

Iwazu!: Hamlet's Satori and Sophie's Choice

The monk Zangen asked, "In this coffin is there life or death?"
Master Dogo replied: "Iwazu! I won't say."

WHEN WE TAKE THE PRECEPTS during ordination, it is not like taking the vows of marriage. You are expected to keep your marriage vows, whether they come naturally or unnaturally, through willing submission or force of will. So they are not exactly just a suggestion of how to proceed. A "suggestion" sounds a bit weak. It is more like, having taken the precepts, "this is now possible." It is like permission to succeed or fail—"thou mayest"—but it is putting all the responsibility on you—"thou mayest just as easily not." It's up to you.

That's what I want to emphasize: taking the precepts is a responsibility you have taken on, but only you know whether you are fulfilling that responsibility. It's like the burden the monk in the story drops to show his awakening on the way down the mountain—what do you do now? You pick it up again and keep going. But now it's *your* burden. It is not something that has been put upon you from on high, or from your parents, or destiny or karma, from outside or over there. It's now something that comes from within.

In Buddhism we talk of two kinds of power: tariki (other power) and jiriki (self power). Many Buddhist sects, such as Pure Land, emphasize tariki, but Zen emphasizes jiriki, the self-motivated power that is most efficacious, most powerful if you're willing to take it on and practice. Other power might come to you through belief alone, but self power comes only through discipline and practice. If it is not spontaneous to begin with, it should become spontaneous. It ensues from earnest discipline and practice.

Take the precept against killing, for example. Is killing wrong? Is killing, as such and in itself, wrong? First, the precept reminds us simply that killing is killing and in most cases, it is wrong. It's a good idea to avoid it. That's the dimension of suggestion. But killing is sometimes necessary. Just make sure you know which is which! Even the Dalai Lama has said that killing is sometimes necessary. If a mosquito is carrying malaria and is about to bite you, you should probably kill it instead of ushering it out the window for it to kill someone else. When he said that, he was not talking about insects; he was not speaking hypothetically. He was speaking analogically, comparing the killing of a dangerous mosquito to the killing of Osama bin Laden. A lot of people were scandalized that he could speak of killing in that way, but he was dead serious.

It's the same thing with the precepts about stealing or abusing sex. It's not that stealing is wrong in and of itself: it might be necessary to steal to prevent a worse outcome. We see this during natural and manmade disasters, where the normal rules are suspended and we have to make decisions based on the situation. We saw this during Katrina in New Orleans, when people found themselves torn between obeying the law against stealing and becoming "looters" to feed themselves and others. It was often so-called looters who saved lives and reduced suffering during that time, doing what needed to be done, which is a good definition of following the Way. Storming the Wal-Mart on Tchoupitoulas for a case of Wild Turkey and a flat-screen TV is looting; taking cases of bottled water, canned tuna, and diapers is doing what needs to be done.

It's not that sex is wrong, it's that sometimes it's unnecessary. When it is unnecessary, superfluous, done on a whim or for purely selfish reasons, it is likely to be more trouble than it's worth—if not for you then for someone else. This is especially true of sex because sex is a giant boulder of karma teetering precariously on a mountaintop. It can only roll down the mountain, causing an avalanche of consequences, which in addition to the immediate agony or ecstasy, may also entail disease and pregnancy, as well as jealousy, attachment, and a whole host of other feelings both good and bad.

Whatever situation you find yourself in, please consider whether an action that contradicts the precepts is necessary—and consider this not with your brain but with your whole being. If you consider the question only with your brain, you can talk yourself into just about anything. You can tell yourself, "Well, sex at this moment might be kind of interesting, kind of fun, might even have a good outcome, maybe it's just what is needed by the cosmos." You can tell yourself, "The road of excess leads to the palace of wisdom," and so forth. I suspect that it is just this sort of parsing of the precepts that gets even some Zen teachers into trouble sometimes; they talk themselves into acting against the precepts, convincing themselves that they are actually doing this for a greater good, to tear down the ego of the student, or other such bad faith bullshit.

Thinking too much can be just as bad as thinking too little. You are just as likely to talk yourself into an unethical action as you are to talk yourself out of one. That's why we need zazen to guide us. And not just to guide us—because zazen will not tell us directly what to do—but actually prepare us by emptying us of our selfish desires and leaving us with mushotoku mind, an attitude of no personal gain or goal, which is precisely the ground upon which all of the precepts are built.

Hamlet is a good case study of thinking too much. Trained as a philosopher at Wittenberg, he was a graduate student well into his early thirties. Scrupulous to a fault, he was incapable of action, and his inability to act caused more harm than an early rash act would have done. Finally, in Act V, when he returns to Denmark from England, it is clear that he returns enlightened because now he can act without thinking too much about it. In England he was supposed to have been murdered and, in a sense, he did die to his former life only to emerge with no fear. Notice that he reappears at the beginning of Act V in a graveyard. He is resurrected. Having climbed into his coffin and come back to life, he knows exactly what needs to be done because he has died to himself. Earlier he had killed the sententious Polonius behind the arras; now he has killed the Polonius in himself, his thinking, always chattering, long-winded brain. He has graduated from the condition of conducting his life through consideration, reflection, rumination. Now he can act with his whole heart, spontaneously, naturally, automatically, authentically. Now we are ready to hear what he is ready to deliver, that wonderful speech about the time being ripe, readiness being all, and the providence that is in the fall of a sparrow.

All this may seem paradoxical. Someone said recently, "So many things point to the fact that discussion and rumination are just distractions. That's why I love coming and doing zazen because there is no romanticism, none of all the stuff your brain can come up with. It's just sitting. It's funny because even with mushotoku mind it's the same thing because you have it in your head." If you just have mushotoku in your head, though, you don't have it. If it's a goal—even if that goal is a lack of a goal, even if the goal is mushotoku itself—it's not mushotoku. When we are sitting, that's what we do. When we're talking, that's what we're doing. *Shikan-taza* and then *Shikan*-talking. Just sitting and then just talking. That's okay too, as long as you do it with mushotoku mind. Ruminate with mushotoku mind and discuss with mushotoku mind. That way you're not trying to impress anyone; you're having an authentic discussion because you have no goal. As long as you have no goal it's mushotoku.

It's not like you're trying to seduce someone or get someone's vote. Politics for the most part is not mushotoku, whether it is political politics or sexual politics. It's important not to push discussion or rumination away as being unproductive or undesirable, just as we should not push reading or thinking away. Remember: in zazen we neither chase after thoughts nor push them away, and it should be the same with intellectual discussions or study. Just let these really be discussion or rumination, or intellectual pursuits, and don't let these rule the roost. *Shikan*-discussion, *shikan*-rumination, *shikan*-intellectualizing. All of these are part of our larger practice. But we always come back to the foundation of shikantaza.

Question: *This is why I bring things up in mondo. Like when I brought up Buddha nature and you said that it was not some "thing" like a soul but just the conditions we have in common with all things that suffer and die.*

Right. It's not a bad thing to state these doubts. What's bad is when you don't say something, thinking that not saying anything shows you're enlightened. That's faking it, that's self-importance. It's simple. If you have something to say, say it. If you have a question, ask it. Blake said, "Always speak your mind and a base man will avoid you." Same thing outside the dojo: if you have something to say, say it. Get into the fray. That's what we do here. We're not a monastic practice withdrawing into the misty mountains. Sometimes we might think that no action would be better than any action. That's what Hamlet thought. When the *Shinjinmei* says just don't decide, just don't choose, it doesn't mean not to do anything. It means that you already know what to do by not thinking about it. That's what we mean by the discipline. In our practice we front-end the decision-making process—or rather we front-end the "not-decision-making" process so that we don't have to be uncertain when the time comes to act. We know what needs to be done.

Question: *So tying it back to the responsibility of the precepts, it sounds to me like it all comes back to returning to the discipline, returning to the practice.*

That's right. Of course it's possible that you might make the wrong decision. It might not affect you the way you would like it to affect you or your loved ones. Still, it might be the right decision because you don't always have a real choice. There might be no "right" decision. It's like a koan, the best kind of koan. There is no right answer to a real koan; there can only be an authentic answer for that time and place and person. The problem is we measure the rightness of our action by the outcome, teleologically, when the outcome cannot be measured by any standard at all because it is transcendent of all human experience.

It's like the novel *Sophie's Choice*. Sophie is a Polish mother who is taken to a Nazi concentration camp, and a Nazi officer tells her that she has to choose which of her two children will live, the son or the daughter. "I can't choose, I can't choose, I can't choose." This is a great koan. (The monk Zangen asked, "In this coffin is there life or death?" And Master Dogo replied: "*Iwazu!* I won't say!") The Nazi starts to take both of them, so she makes a spontaneous decision, but she is wracked with guilt for the rest of her life because even though she saved the son she feels that she sent the daughter to her death. Which would have been better? Not to choose and let both of them die? Or to choose one and send the other to her death? How do you get past the responsibility for that? Put in that situation what would you do? That's a good koan for anyone to wrestle with because there is no good answer, no right answer. But you might be able to come up with an authentic answer if you really face the question with your whole being.

But to go back to the responsibility endowed on us by the precepts by "thou mayest," taking responsibility doesn't mean taking on the guilt. It means doing the only thing you can do.

Question: *We all carry around so much baggage, dust. We learn how we act under certain situations, sometimes not so well. It's those mindless sorts of self-harm and harm to others that we have to take responsibility for, it seems to me. What is our responsibility for that, and what does it mean? If you are mindless about those things, how can you not take responsibility for them?*

By all means, take responsibility, but don't overthink it. Mindfulness too often becomes just being aware that you're thinking about your responsibility all the time. Like, should I do dishes now or later, now or later, now or later? That doesn't get you anywhere. You could have done the dishes and had a second helping of dessert in the meantime. That is just obsession, preoccupation, more of the same. I prefer to think of this attitude as "right *mindlessness*." Just get your mind out of it. Don't be thinking about it all the time. I remember bringing up a similar question, like yours, to my teacher long ago in terms of consciousness or awareness, and he said just don't worry about consciousness or awareness. What we think of as mindfulness or self-awareness is often just self-congratulation: "I am mindful about what I am eating, what a good boy am I!"

I was at a conference in San Diego recently and ate at a fancy restaurant with a fabulous view, above a Lexus dealership. I had ordered a vegetarian dish in advance with the conference registration, but when I got there I thought, "Gee, I don't really want a vegetarian meal tonight." I wanted the chicken, which sounded great. And when those fragrant quarters of poultry started arriving in front of other diners, I was right: it looked great and it smelled great, and I'm convinced it tasted great. If I had been enlightened (or just a little more assertive), I would have canceled my order on the spot, claiming that I had been converted from vegetarianism since placing my order several months before, and demanded my fair share of that aromatic chicken. Instead, I was being just a little too mindful (i.e., self-congratulatory), maybe even a little self-righteous because I thought a vegetarian meal would be good for me. As it turned out, I got some bean soup no doubt prepared by a chef with a grudge against vegetarians, and everyone else got a real meal.

Question: *We've got all this memory, this samsara that makes us what we are today. If we are acting in some way that's not working for us, it seems worthwhile to become conscious of the past, the baggage and what makes us act that way. That does seem mental but it also seems worthwhile.*

But how did you get to that point, where you could see the situation in that light, see that this is constructed and not necessary behavior? How did you see that it was samsara at work and not who you are, not your identity? You got there by sitting, not by thinking it out in your head. That reflective part is a mental process, sure. You're deconstructing what has been constructed and you're making something new. It's not necessarily mindfulness, it's just the examined life that's worth living. You can call it mindfulness if you like, but true mindfulness is what you're doing before you're aware of mindfulness. When you're aware of being mindful it's not mindfulness anymore. Once you name it, it disappears.

As my teacher always said, "Think with the body, act with the mind." So that when your mind is acting, the body goes directly into action. When the body is thinking, the thought manifests. The problem is we think with the mind too much instead of thinking as one integrated, whole person. It's like small boys who act with the body without thinking with it: they throw themselves against the walls without knowing quite sure why. Our minds are often like small boys, flinging themselves against the furniture without thinking. When we think and act with the whole person, with body-mind, we don't contradict what needs to be done. Too often we do what we *think* or *feel* needs to be done instead. "Even though my body wants to do that, I'm going to do this because my mind thinks I should." But if our mind is attuned with our body, and our body is attuned with our mind, we have no choice.

Is it the right time to think? Think! Do it because it's your whole body thinking. This is what koans are about. Koans can't be figured out with your head. This is what happened with Sophie. She could not make her decision on any rational basis. Faced with having to make a decision, she acted with her body when she reached out and grabbed one of her kids. But she was never reconciled with that because she always thought she had a choice. Sophie never had a choice! Therefore she didn't have to take responsibility for that action, yet she did have to take responsibility for that action. This is what a koan is. "Thou mayest." A beautiful thing. A beautiful tragedy.

Sophie's Choice is a good example of a certain dissonance, a lack of resolution to some problems, that comes with our practice. Even though she wasn't responsible, she took responsibility. She was forever attached to the guilt associated with her action. She became that guilt; she became that action instead of the totality of the actions in her life. Sophie didn't have the mechanism to deal with the responsibility that comes with "thou mayest." She didn't have the practice that would have got her past it. Maybe we can't get past certain things in our life at all. Her suicide is like the seppuku of the samurai who has taken on the responsibility for his actions, including the karma and samsara that he has inherited, even though there was nothing else he could have done to avoid it.

That said, I think you can get past just about anything. When we think about a tragedy, when we think about the death of a loved one, for example, we might think we could never get over that. It just seems impossible. Yet people do get past such events, even if they never get over them. Knowing that this can happen, that mujo can strike at any time is very valuable for our practice. Knowing that mujo can strike, we have to ask how do we live our lives now? How do we make our lives meaningful? What do we do to quicken our life, to make it important, and not just let it slip by? If what happened to Sophie should happen to us, what would we do? What would you do?

When we look at our lives, though, aren't we actually confronted with Sophie's Choice at every moment? What do we see but loss, loss, loss? Instead of doing what needs to be done, though, we react like the pre-Act V Hamlet and just think about it, putting off the decisions, justifying our reluctance with a host of scruples, hoping like Eliot's Prufrock that we have the time to "murder and create," when actually we need only to do what needs to be done.

Fox Zen and Hound Zen

One law for the lion and the ox is oppression.
—William Blake

IF YOU HAVE EVER played Fox and Hounds, you know what I mean. All you need to play is a checkerboard and five checkers, four black for the Hounds and one red for the Fox. The Fox can move diagonally in any direction, while the Hounds can move only diagonally forward. For the Hounds, the object is to corner the Fox. To win, the Hounds must be methodical and stick to their patterned behavior. They run in packs, so any variation can trip up their coordinated effort. Any slip-up will be capitalized upon by the Fox whose sole object is to evade the methodical Hounds and break through to the other side.

This game is a good parable for two types of Zen. Hound Zen moves in one direction, bound strictly by the rules of the game. It follows the precepts straightforwardly. Hounds shave their heads, eat no meat, abstain from all alcohol and sex, etc. Often they bark at others who don't follow their regimen, such as the Fox. In Fox Zen there is no path that's straight and narrow. Fox Zen moves backward and forward and sideways, bound by a single precept: get to the other side. Fox Zen lays low and often outside the kennels where Hound Zen is penned. Foxes are invisible to the naked eye and nose. Their musky odor cloaks them; they stink but not of Zen. You might glimpse Foxes in public, but they don't heel to the command of hunters as Hounds do. They are ghosts.

Fox Zen and Hound Zen are not two, though. Fox Zen and Hound Zen are in each of us who practice. While the drama between the two can sometimes play out between different individuals in a sangha or between sanghas, the real game is played by two sides of the same person. We all have a Fox and many Hounds within us. The Fox roams freely and sometimes fearfully. The Hounds gravitate to groups and find a nervous solace there. Our Hound nature sees the Fox as dangerous and disruptive to the greater order. The Fox sees the Hounds as lickspittles and slaves. But it is not the iconoclastic practitioner or teacher who is the threat to the Hounds; it is the Hounds' own inner Fox that they fear and that they hope to subdue by sticking strictly to ritual, precepts, and institutional structures. The more the Fox bobs and weaves, the more the Hounds will howl to box him in, demanding that he too must play by their rules and limitations. The more the Hounds slaver and drool with their noses to the ground in pursuit of the invisible Fox at the sound of the hunter's horn, the more the Fox will leap and dance to music only the Fox can hear.

Observe, though, the Fox and Hounds in their original state. At the beginning of the game there is no Fox and there are no Hounds. There are only checkers sitting on their black squares, zafus on zabutons. There is no Fox Zen and no Hound Zen. There is only zazen.

III

The Way of

Bodhisattva Strategy

Commentary on Miyamoto Musashi's Dokkodo

With respect for Michael Flachmann (1942–2013)

Fear no more the heat o' the sun,

Nor the furious winter's rages;

Thou thy worldly task hast done,

Home art gone, and ta'en thy wages;

Golden lads and girls all must,

As chimney-sweepers, come to dust.

Fear no more the frown o' the great,

Thou art past the tyrant's stroke:

Care no more to clothe and eat;

To thee the reed is as the oak:

The scepter, learning, physic, must

All follow this, and come to dust.

Cymbeline (4.2)

INTRODUCTION

Whole Heart Abandonment

MUSASHI'S DOKKODO, WRITTEN DAYS before his death for his disciple Terao Magonojo, is a list of pronouncements, "thou-shalt-nots," that can be taken as monastic precepts for the aspiring warrior, as Terao took them and as generations of Musashi's followers have taken them. They are tenets of a practice that can be thought of, the title says, as "The Way to Be Followed Alone." Although the "way of strategy" is his way, Musashi does not see this way as so narrow that it would be inapplicable to a wider audience. In the following commentary I outline how "the way of strategy" can be largely relevant to bodhisattva practice. Like the warrior, the lay or bodhisattva practitioner's path is through this world, engaged and, more often than not, embattled. The way of bodhisattva strategy, then, is the way that does not shy away from worldly conflicts but rather enters into worldly conflicts to find the best resolution possible. The way of bodhisattva strategy is a way of harmonizing with our immediate surroundings, humanity, and the cosmos. For this reason Musashi's *Dokkodo* is implicitly related to true Zen practice.

Thanks to Musashi's broad vision, I believe these commentaries can—by elucidating or elaborating upon his brief insights—prove useful to all Zen practitioners, but perhaps especially to those lineages that, like Taisen Deshimaru's, have retained a trace of the samurai spirit and tradition.

As Kodo Sawaki points out in his "Talks on the *Shodoka*," Musashi's *Dokkodo* exemplifies "the vivid life-attitude of Zen itself [that] became the Japanese samurai." For Sawaki, Budo Zen or Samurai Zen showed "a very clear enlightenment," the Zen of no fear.

Some American Zen groups, on the other hand, while quite rightly distancing themselves from the militaristic and patriarchal past of Japanese Zen, have also rejected the uncompromising discipline and the complex code of honor of the samurai that have fortified (some would say tainted) some strains of Japanese Zen. Many have also dropped such appurtenances as the kyosaku, the "wake-up" stick, as inappropriate to a democratic and enlightened 21st-century practice. While they may have a point in the use of the kyosaku as rensaku, or "education stick," a practice difficult to justify in a contemporary context, the kyosaku remains pertinent less for its symbolism as the sword that cuts illusion than for its usefulness in jolting the body-mind awake during zazen. The samurai tradition is not all violence and blind devotion; above all it believes in discipline in and out of the dojo, devotion to a code of loyalty and sacrifice, the inseparability of the body-mind, and the futility of attachment not only to the material comforts of this life but to life itself. Anyone who appreciates these principles in Musashi will grasp their value for bodhisattva practice even in a time of peace.

Musashi approached the work of writing the *Dokkodo*, like other revelators (we call them prophets), as a sacred act. Like Mohammed and St. John, Musashi went into a cave to perform his act of contemplative composition. Like Moses, Musashi gives us a list of commandments in the form of "thou-shalt-nots" (at least this repetitive form is what is arbitrarily chosen by the translator of Kenji Tokitsu's *Miyamoto Musashi: His Life and Writings*, the text I have used here). As Kodo Sawaki says, "In reading the *Dokkodo*, one sees that even though it is very short, every sentence is to the point." Unlike Moses, John, or Mohammed, however, Musashi had no illusions that his revelations were divine; nor are his injunctions moralistic. In spirit they are more like the *Meditations* of Marcus Aurelius, useful reflections from a Stoic soldier on how to live a sober life for the greater good, without any thought of personal reward, gleaned from vast experience in the way of strategy, and put down on paper as a record of his realizations.

The tone is not avuncular; it is oracular. We hear the crisp bark of aphorisms distilled from Musashi's long intimacy with and intense devotion to his art, the art of the warrior. But Musashi allowed that all arts are related and that to know the essentials of one is to understand the heart of all others because each of the arts is a footpath along the great Way:

> We may speak of the way of the Confucians, of the Buddhists, of tea masters, of masters of etiquette, or of dancers, but these ways are distinct from the way of the warrior. Nonetheless, anyone who understands the way in great depth will find the same principle in all things. It is important for each person to persevere in his own way. (147)

This insistence on the creativity and originality of the individual speaks to us today far more than his insistence on following tradition, even though both are necessary for the way of strategy. Musashi is no slave to tradition or to form, but he does not neglect or disrespect them either. Like many great swordsmen with experience in battle, like George Silver or Sir Richard F. Burton, Musashi is interested in what works in real- life conflicts (i.e., on the field of life and death) rather than in form for form's sake. He is a duelist, not a fencer; a bodhisattva warrior, not a parish priest.

In the end, the measure of our practice must not be whether we live up to the pronouncements of a renowned master or whether we can parrot the insights of a famous work, however inspired. In the end, the measure of our practice is what we are able to do in the life-and-death struggles of everyday life. In *The Zen Way to the Martial Arts* and elsewhere, Taisen Deshimaru speaks eloquently of the samurai tradition and its relevance to Zen practice, so I don't intend to repeat what he says here. I do, however, want to help adapt what is relevant in our 21st-century Zen practice in America to this tradition, while allowing what is not relevant, like rensaku, to atrophy and fall off. For many years to come, American Buddhists will continue to digest the traditions of our Japanese, Chinese, Vietnamese, Korean, or Tibetan lineages, keeping what we can stomach and rejecting what we cannot. This is natural in the evolution and migration of any species, religion, language, or culture. Each will make whatever adjustments are necessary to adapt to the demands and conditions of the here and now. This is not a problem; it is an opportunity to act freely with all our faculties without thought of our own reward but for the greater good, making our presence on the path not a hindrance but a moment of celebration. Musashi's advice can be useful for this modest, heroic purpose, and it is in this spirit that my commentaries are offered.

Text of Miyamoto Musashi's Dokkodo

Translated by Sherab Chodzin Kohn
in *Miyamoto Mushashi: His Life and Writings*
(Weatherhill, 2006)

1 *Do not go against the way of the world that is perpetuated from generation to generation.*

2 *Do not seek pleasure for its own sake.*

3 *Do not, in any circumstance, depend upon a partial feeling.*

4 *Think lightly of yourself and think deeply of the world.*

5 *Be detached from desire your whole life long.*

6 *Do not regret what you have done.*

7 *Never be jealous of others, either in good or in evil.*

8 *Never let yourself be saddened by a separation.*

9 *Resentment and complaint are appropriate neither for yourself nor for others.*

10 *Do not let yourself be guided by love.*

11 *In all things, do not have any preferences.*

12 *Do not have any particular desire regarding your private domicile.*

13 *Do not pursue the taste of good food.*

14 *Do not possess ancient objects intended to be preserved for the future.*

15 *Do not follow customary beliefs.*

16 *Do not seek especially either to collect or to practice arms beyond what is useful.*

17 *Do not shun death in the way.*
18 *Do not seek to possess either goods or fiefs for your old age.*
19 *Respect Buddha and the gods without counting on their help.*
20 *You can abandon your own body, but you must hold on to your honor.*
21 *Never stray from the way of strategy.*

Commentary on Miyamoto Musashi's Dokkodo

1 "Do not go against the way of the world that is perpetuated from generation to generation."

This precept is often translated—and truncated—to read, "Accept everything just the way it is." This is a mistake. This violates both the letter and the spirit of Musashi who, as a warrior, accepts what has been established by long tradition and his role in that lineage. There is a vast difference between accepting "everything just the way it is," which is quietism, and not going against the way things have been arranged by dint of tradition, which is a bow—a gesture of respect and humility. The latter attitude accepts the reality of the way things are because these are the conditions under which we work but understands that the way things are is not an absolute Way (not the Tao) but only the relative way of the world (convention). Conditions must be accepted but conventions can be changed. One must accept the rules of the game passed down by tradition, but one can only adjust one's actions according to those rules if one is still going to influence the outcome of the conflict. Going against the rules of the game can only end in defeat. Going against the way of the world will only end in suffering.

Musashi's opening edict does not mean that we should conform mindlessly to societal demands or expectations. We know this because later on he will assert, "Do not act following customary beliefs" (#15). When it comes to following or deviating from others' expectations, we choose our battles. We acknowledge the conditions under which we work and the repercussions of going against the grain. We do not reinvent the rules of the game as we play it. We do not try to reinvent the world according to our idea of the way things "should" be. Once we begin down the road of "should," the choices never end, the suffering never ends.

There is an Asian mourning custom of not making any changes in the way one does things for a year after the death of a father. This practice is extended in the practice of some Zen lineages. There was a period when I left my master for five years. Even after leaving, though, I did not change the practice or his teaching. After five years, when I suddenly showed up in the dojo again, he accepted me back without hesitation, saying, "I could tell it was you by your posture." Even in the dimly lit dojo, even with his diminished sight, he could see by my posture that I had not betrayed his teaching. I may have left his presence but his influence never left me. His teaching was intact. Now, at eighty-one years old, his teaching is still strong, and if I outlive him I will not willfully change the practice as he taught it to me.

Change exerts itself on us enough gradually through time, memory loss, and circumstance without our changing things up intentionally just to suit our ideas about what might work better. Most of our ideas about changing a practice that has been established for generations, while well intentioned, have unintended results. Things change, with or without us. A year's cooling-off period is a good way to allow any ideas about improving on a generations-old practice to pass, letting the initial seductive heat of inspiration chill into a better, less self-serving change, namely the kind of change that in any case takes years through a process that is natural and gradual, evolutionary not revolutionary. Most proposed changes will be abandoned altogether with such a cooling-off period. The human world, like the natural world, evolves whether we like it or not. Our wishes are, to a certain extent, irrelevant. The human world, like the natural world, has evolved into its current expression of the Way, and it is our sole duty to find how we can best contribute not to reinventing the Way but to harmonizing with it.

In the human world, this sometimes appears to mean "accepting things just as they are," but really it means "accepting the way of the world as it has been perpetuated from generation to generation." Sometimes harmonizing means adhering to laws and to the social contract that might not always suit us, but sometimes adhering to our code of honor means going against the way of the world. At those times, we must accept the fact that we can't have it both ways. If we can't accept the way of the world and adhere to our code, the samurai code of death before dishonor comes in handy. As Musashi puts it, "You can abandon your own body, but you must hold on to your honor" (#20). You cannot betray a trust and be a hero. You cannot stand up for a principle and evade the consequences for doing so. We all function within social agreements that existed well before us. We did not ask for the conditions into which we are born, nor the conditions under which we work, but that does not mean that we have the right to contravene them at will. These conditions are fluid: they continue to change, and we continue to change with them, if we are able. If we are not able to change them, we may have difficulty adapting to new conditions, and like any species that does not adapt, we will not survive. For the bodhisattva, like the warrior, the first duty is to survive, for which knowing the conditions of survival that have come down to us generation after generation is crucial. If one cannot survive with both body and honor intact, a choice must be made.

2 "Do not seek pleasure for its own sake."

Seeking pleasure for its own sake, especially the pleasures of the body but also the pleasures of the mind, is self-defeating. Once one begins to pursue the preference for pleasure, there is no end to pleasure seeking. Only pain can follow the path of endless pleasure, as Epicurus realized. Like other post-Socratic philosophies, Epicureanism has been given a bad name, having entered into popular parlance not as a philosophy of balance but as a synonym for "gourmet" or "gourmand." Epicurus believed it was natural to seek the good and that pleasure was the way we naturally identify the good; thus it was natural to seek pleasure and to avoid pain. Like the Buddha, he also knew that the extremes of pleasure and pain are equally undesirable, and so he sought balance, the Middle Path. By avoiding the pendulum swing of pleasure/pain, the Epicurean—like the Cynic, the Stoic, and the Skeptic in their own ways—maximizes the "pleasure" of the Middle Path.

This precept is not a simple moralistic imperative against pleasure as a sin, since pleasure is not an evil in itself, something to be ashamed of, or even regretted (#6 tells us to regret nothing). Musashi is not, as some have asserted, a masochist or an ascetic (his self-denials have a pragmatic purpose, not a crypto-hedonistic one—not the moralist's "self enjoyings of self denial" to be found in hypocrite religion, as Blake puts it in *Visions of the Daughters of Albion*). Musashi would, like a good Stoic, argue that one should avoid equally the extremes of both pleasure and pain, or rather that one should avoid neither pleasure nor pain. In this way, Musashi's Middle Path is stricter than the Epicurean's who would above all seek pleasure by avoiding pain. It is not pleasure or pain in itself that should be avoided but preferences of all sorts. So we should interpret this precept precisely: "Neither seek pleasure, nor avoid pain." Why seek them out when they will come on their own, whether we will or no.

This does not mean, however, that we should deprive ourselves of pleasures that ensue from our various other pursuits that are done for "their own sake," such as doing good work, practicing the discipline of our lives, and helping others. And what of the other, everyday pleasures of enjoying the weather, good company, exercise, food and drink? Even relaxation and "down time" are as necessary as sleep for the rejuvenation of the muscles and the sanity of the mind to balance our lives and prepare us for whatever comes. These too, since they are not necessarily sought out for their own sake but enjoyed along the way and as part of a larger definition of training and discipline, are not to be despised but to be enjoyed thoroughly and without regret.

3 *"Do not, in any circumstance, depend upon a partial feeling."*
Most of us are at the mercy of our whims. One of the many things the discipline of zazen teaches us is that we can sit through both the distractions of our body and the distractions

of our minds. Even though we are uncomfortable, or we feel the urge to scratch an itch, or we wish we could stretch that muscle when a charley horse attacks it, we continue to sit undisturbed on a deep level. Likewise, when our minds pull us this way and that, we notice this, we notice that, but we don't get up, we fix our gaze, we keep our posture, we exhale in a long, slow, deep way, concentrated on posture and breathing because it is posture and breathing that we are acting on wholeheartedly. Even though we have a halfhearted desire to get up, fix ourselves a bowl of ice cream and stretch out in the hammock for a long summer morning's nap, we continue zazen.

I have made some big mistakes in life by acting on what I thought were wholehearted feelings, but most of my mistakes (at least the ones I have regretted) were decisions that I made upon partial feelings. Beginning Zen practice was not one of them. Zen requires that we throw ourselves into the practice with a whole heart. It is just as important to act this way in anything we do, with urgency and complete devotion, "as though our hair is on fire." If we love our children in this way, choose our profession in this way, buy houses in this way, marry in this way—we may still make mistakes but we are unlikely to suffer regrets, since there is nothing else we could have done, and we will not be haunted by the road not taken even if the road taken was not all we cracked it up to be.

Acting wholeheartedly, though, is easier said than done. We are used to seeing things circumspectly, eyeing them from various angles. This is the value but also the downfall of rational thinking, indeed of philosophy, of philosophical thinking, of comparative religion, of critical thinking. These habits of mind can risk rendering us useless, like Hamlet, without convictions, unable to act, or (which is even worse) sending us into a halfhearted action that the thinking brain has weighed, calculating profit and loss, and approved. The value of zazen is that it suspends rational thinking—or rather that it *transcends* rational thinking—putting our discriminating mind on hold so that we can discover the wholehearted realm of the natural (the Way), the automatic, the spontaneous action of the whole heart. Zen practice allows us to discover not so much our identity as our integrity, where our whole heart lies. This is the "heart wisdom" of true integrity that we voice every day when we chant the *Heart Sutra*, taking us out of the realm of the merely perceived or conceived, the merely felt or thought, and into beyond the beyond. Where is "beyond the beyond"? The great here and now.

4 *"Think lightly of yourself and think deeply of the world."*
As we put down the pursuit of halfhearted pleasures, we begin to center ourselves outside ourselves, not in our id or ego (our appetites for pleasure or pride) but in the real world, where infinite value resides. This decentered self is central to the bodhisattva way. As Shantideva puts it in *Guide to the Bodhisattva Life*, all joy comes from thinking of others, all suffering from thinking of oneself. But it is not just *what* we are thinking about ("ourselves" and "the world") but *how* we think about these objects ("lightly" and "deeply").

Oscar Wilde, who subtitled his famous play *The Importance of Being Earnest* "A Trivial Comedy for Serious People," said to his friend Robert Ross, "We should treat all trivial things very seriously, and all the serious things of life with sincere and studied triviality." And in the *Hagakure*, a hundred years after Musashi and a hundred years before Wilde, Yamamoto

Tsunetomo wrote: "Matters of great concern should be treated lightly....Matters of small concern should be treated seriously." Tsunetomo was quoting Master Itei, but he could as well have been thinking of Musashi. He elaborates on how one is able to approach matters in this counterintuitive way, not by neglecting the great concerns or spending little time or effort on them but first by keeping their number small and then by considering them with such diligence "during normal times" before they need to be acted upon that once the need to act on them arises, one is ready, "resolved beforehand," and can act without hesitation. Thus the samurai attitude is not exactly the same as Oscar Wilde's witty paradox, but Wilde was as dead serious as any samurai when it came to the serious care to be taken with such supposedly superficial or trivial matters as posture, the cut of a coat, accessorizing with walking-sticks or green carnations, or how to wear rouge in the attitude of the metaphysical dandy.

Attainment is ever indirect. Rarely when we go after something directly—through the will alone—can we attain it. Attainment comes unconsciously, automatically, naturally, spontaneously, if we have prepared properly. The debate between the Southern and Northern Schools, or between sudden and gradual enlightenment, offers a false choice. In the *Hagakure*, gradual preparation leads to sudden, spontaneous action. We find this in Zen practice: constant daily practice (*gyoji*) leads to authentic spontaneity. Deshimaru tells the story of a samurai who gave his obeisance to Hachiman, bodhisattva of budo, and upon coming out of the sanctuary sensed the presence of a monster which he slew "unconsciously." "Intuition and action must spring forth at the same time," Deshimaru concludes. "In the practice of budo there can be no conscious thought. There is no time for thinking, not even an instant. When a person acts, intention and action must be simultaneous...This is hishiryo consciousness" (*The Zen Way to the Martial Arts*, 17). It is no different for the bodhisattva in everyday practice. Even in everyday matters that are not matters of life and death, we can unite intention and action for the utmost benefit of all beings.

We prepare the soil for planting, set the stage, save for a rainy day, train for battle. Pick your metaphor. Musashi's wisdom on this matter concerns the nature of indirect as opposed to direct attainment. You do not drop off body and mind by trying to drop off body and mind, just as you don't find love by looking for it. (You might find something but it is unlikely to be love.) Dogen says, "To study the self is to forget the self," and vice versa. In zazen we don't concentrate on dropping anything off; we don't concentrate on attaining enlightenment. We concentrate on posture and breathing. If self drops off, it is an indirect attainment, not something that can be successfully sought and attained directly with conscious effort.

The humanist psychologist Viktor Frankl said that we Americans have an odd notion in our *Declaration of Independence*, claiming a right to life, liberty, and the "pursuit of happiness." "You cannot pursue happiness," he writes in *Man's Search for Meaning* (1946); "it must ensue, and it only does so as the unintended side effect of one's personal dedication to a cause greater than oneself or as the byproduct of one's surrender to a person other than oneself." Once the decentered self is devoted to a cause outside itself, the possibility of happiness arises spontaneously and unconsciously. This comes indirectly from treating trivial things seriously and serious things lightly, and treating the world deeply and ourselves lightly.

Likewise, as Dogen knew, and Musashi too, when we study the world, we discover ourselves. When we contemplate the world deeply, the burden of ourselves lifts, and we can laugh at ourselves. This is true "en*light*enment," a "lightening" that has nothing to do with lumens but rather with ounces, not with illumination but with losing weight, what Milan Kundera so aptly called the "unbearable lightness of being." When the lightness of being is unbearable (*dhukka*), we are on the brink of throwing down body and mind (satori). When we have thrown down body and mind, the heaviness of being becomes bearable.

5 "Be detached from desire your whole life long."

In English "desire" can be relatively mild like a longing, wish, or passing whim, or relatively intense, like an obsession or addiction. The word for desire here, *yokushin*, suggests specifically selfish wishes, lusts, or cupidity, that greediness for physical pleasure or material accumulation that resists control. It could also apply to greediness for spiritual or intellectual pleasure, or experiential accumulation, all of which are caricatures of those tepid desires we call *preferences*.

To be "detached from desire" might give a wrong impression. In Buddhist thought "non-attachment" is not the same as "detachment." Being detached implies an attitude of indifference, and certainly Musashi would have his samurai indifferent to the tugs of desire. But non-attachment implies a more thorough and paradoxical immunity to desire, one that would allow participation in the desire with a simultaneous uninvolvement. There is a kind of desire that implies no sense of attachment, only a healthy striving, as in having a "desire for world peace." A "lust" or "obsession" for world peace, however, we would agree sounds harmful. These are forms of attachment to a specific goal, the frustrations of which can be dangerous, and this is what yokushin implies.

Since desire is by definition a state of living outside of the present, it asserts that reality is inadequate, incomplete. Indeed, philosophers often note that "desire is a lack." A lack is felt *as* a lack, "lack" being the function of the assertion of a wished-for or desired presence, followed by, or simultaneous with, recognition of an absence. Lack or absence is not the same as emptiness (sunyata or ku). A lack is, we might say, an emptiness full of the absence of something, thus not truly empty, not ku. Such an emptiness is not emptiness at all—it is, rather, a ghost. The absence-in-presence haunts us. It is this present-absence (or presence-in-absence) that disturbs us in the form of desire. But desire is a ghost, an apparition, a wraith, unreal, illusion.

This realization is reinforced in #8: "Never let yourself be saddened by a separation." Separations whether by travel or death are the very demonstration of presence-in-absence. When we miss someone, something is missing from our lives in the moment. But it is only seen as missing if we look for it there and it is not to be found.

We do this all the time in our lives. We look for a quality in our mate and, not finding it there, we "miss" it, seeing it as a lack and therefore as something to be desired. In our job, we fantasize about how things should be, projecting the ideal into the real, allowing the real to be haunted by the ghost of the ideal (i.e., the unreal, the illusory). Thus we allow ourselves to be disturbed by the separation or gap between the way things "should" be and the way they are. We allow ourselves to be haunted by ghosts.

Non-attachment presupposes that we have defused the disappointment that comes of separation anxiety. I use this developmental term purposely because we all revert to a childish state when threatened by the insecurities associated with separation, especially from those things we think we desire or can't live without. This is particularly evident in hoarders, whose problems usually have their origins in a neurotic response to separation resulting in a deep attachment to things which provide a momentary, tenuous, and insatiable desire to fill a bottomless lack, an endless desire to accumulate and control the threat of separation, to resurrect and collect ghosts.

6 "Do not regret what you have done."

Regret is another form of attachment. By holding on to regrets we believe that we can somehow control the past. By filing something away or interpreting it as regret, we fool ourselves into thinking that our regrets will prevent us from acting in similar ways again, thereby preventing similar mistakes in the future. In reality, regrets keep us chained to past patterns and ensure that we will act in similar ways again because *that's who we are* (or so our attachments tell us).

Why else do regrets tend to multiply rather than diminish the more we hold onto them? Because regrets help us to form an identity to which we cling. We *are* our mistakes, and as much as we might like to convince ourselves that we are *better* than our actions or the sum total of our mistakes, regret is our way of anchoring our identity firmly in those actions. By identifying with the action, we think we own it—actually, it owns us. When regret owns us, we are lost to that attachment.

How do we drop such attachment? As we drop all attachments: by doing zazen. By sitting and existing completely in the present moment during zazen we practice being nonattached; we confront the emptiness (not the lack) of our own identity. Such emptiness is not a loss, not a lack; such emptiness is pure potential and complete achievement. Only in realizing the emptiness of ourselves do we meet our true selves. Unlike a lack, which is a prison (the prison of desire), emptiness is pure freedom and entire accomplishment.

Regret is that lack, that prison, a caricature of yourself. Casting off regret, you free yourself of the prison of acting according to the role assigned by past actions. When we speak of throwing down or casting off body and mind, some people envision losing consciousness or awareness, but it is really just losing regret and (regret's future shadow) ambition.

Some Zen teachers speak against the idea of free will, citing the dogma of karma. This is complete nonsense. It is true: karma does restrict our free will. Regret is one form of karma; so is ambition. But we are not helpless in the grip of karma, unless we choose to be. Choosing to practice zazen, we immediately cut our karma by casting off regret and ambition, the ghosts of karma past and karma future, and taking charge of the present. Zazen cuts karma by freeing us of the inertia of karmic velocity. We may not be able to hit the brakes and stop karma on a dime, but if we engage the clutch we can slow down and coast to a stop during zazen.

7 "*Never be jealous of others, either in good or in evil.*"
This is a difficult one to understand mostly because of the "good and evil" qualification. Not to be jealous or envious is clear: such an emotion is patently not being present, not

accepting things as they are. And to be jealous of the good or jealous of the evil would make sense if we are envying the benefits others are harvesting from their "good" or "evil" actions. To be jealous in good or in evil makes less sense. But let this distinction go for now and let's assume that jealous of good or of evil is the intention in Kohn's translation of Musashi's text.

We have all been jealous or envious of the good fortune of others, even when the benefits that they enjoy are due to their own efforts or to luck, to their own virtues or to their own vices. There is even a word for it: *schadenfreude*. That is perhaps the distinction being made—that whatever the source or cause of one's fortune doesn't matter because jealousy itself is already making a distinction. The *Shinjinmei* is right: once you state a preference you are already lost. As I like to put it: "Preferences kill zazen."

To see someone who is successful—especially someone who seems to have started with the same advantages or disadvantages as ourselves—urges us to compare them with us. Why, we ask, are they so fortunate and we so unfortunate? That question in itself is not pernicious: it could lead to an improvement in our plans or our behavior, using them as a model. "Ah, they were thrifty: I will be thriftier." Or, "Ah, they were diligent: I will be more diligent." On the "evil" side, though, it might lead to this: "Ah, they were ruthless: I will be more ruthless." Either way, making these comparisons is in itself pernicious, whether "in good or in evil" qualities.

8 "Never let yourself be saddened by a separation."
This direction will be resisted by those who are confused about the concept of "non-attachment" in Buddhist practice.

In the West we tend to value our attachments, not only to material things (materialism) but to emotional things (sentimentalism), to intellectual things (intellectualism), and to spiritual things (piety). All of these are vices in Musashi's view, and they are impediments to true Zen practice. We might add that an attachment to Buddhist things (or all things Buddhist, including its philosophy) is another vice or impediment (and it is called Buddhism). Not only do we value the things and people and ideas to which we are attached but we find our identity in them: we identify with them. This is fine to a certain extent—these identities and attachments define our social, familial, economic, and political roles and allow us to function usefully in the world. But we should not confuse these roles with our "true face," which is that which precedes all roles and souls: this is the true face of emptiness, where attachment is impossible to sustain because in true emptiness the mirror gazes into the mirror. Which is real and which unreal?

We realize in Zen practice what our true face is, was, and will be. We connect with a consciousness that is pre-separation anxiety, pre-separation individuation, before we have indicated our separate self which is the cause of all our successes but also all of our failures, many of our joys but also most of our sorrows.

If all things are interdependent, then no thing can ever be separate, even if it appears absent. If I am across the room from my daughter, I am not terribly concerned about her distance from me. While I might prefer it when she is sitting next to me, reading, because of the affectionate contact we share, I don't panic when she leaves the chair or the room. But if she leaves the house, I begin to worry. And the farther she goes, the more my worry increases, in part because I feel less in control of any dangers that might come to her. This is natural—it is a non-neurotic attachment and is connected to our instinct for survival. What would not be natural—and would therefore be a neurotic attachment—is if I panicked while she was still in the room, or in the house out of my sight.

This is the narcissistic panic felt by the narrator in Marcel Proust's novel *À la recherche du temps perdu (In Search of Lost Time)*, who panics because his love, Albertine, is sleeping beside him and he is unsure of her dream whereabouts. This is a neurotic attachment that causes him to suffer (and he in turn causes her to suffer) because he has an unreasonable expectation of his ability to control her love for him. Even in her dreams, he is saddened or alarmed by separation—in this case not a physical separation, but a separation nonetheless and emblematic of all separation, since the sadness has nothing to do with the physical but everything to do with one's perception of one's relation to the object of attachment, which in most cases is not physical at all. Even in death, it is not the body we miss but the interaction, the comfort, the reflection of ourselves in the attention given to us by the object (this is true whether it is a person or a possession or a pet). This reflexive mirror of attention is what comforts or disturbs us humans about dogs and disturbs or comforts us about cats.

John Donne's poem "A Valediction: Forbidding Mourning" illustrates the point. The speaker of the poem is doing exactly what Musashi is doing in this precept: forbidding mourning over separation as not only unhealthy but also as a lack of faith in a "higher" connection of souls. For Musashi, it is not very different, except that the higher connection is not in the realm of spiritual love's locus in heaven or God's love, but rather in the realm of existential interdependence, or dependent origination. In a sense, Donne's compass metaphor is a mechanistic image for a much more pervasive connection between all beings.

Of course we will be saddened by separation, whether we "let" ourselves or not. The question is: will we allow ourselves to be defeated by that sadness? Will we, like the hoarder for whom a perverse attachment and accumulation is an attempt to fill an abyss of sadness due to separation, allow ourselves to sink under the weight of sadness and fear, or will we let go of our attachment and free ourselves by emptying what is already empty and embracing that instead of trying to cling to what is insubstantial anyway, what is transient by nature, what is sure to fall away from us in any case? Could there be any more diametrical opposition than the hoarder aesthetic of accumulation and the Zen aesthetic of subtraction?

9 "Resentment and complaint are appropriate neither for yourself nor for others."
Is there anything less pretty than a whiner? Some will make any issue about themselves. They will find endless excuses for why they are unable to achieve some goal, usually because they did not get the support of someone in a more powerful position than they, which may include not being born into a certain stratum of society or being given certain talents by their creator. These are the perpetual losers. Their complaints are boundless. Those who succeed do so no matter how little support they get from others, finding support where none is given, not even from the Buddha or the gods, upon whom we are told we cannot rely—but from themselves.

As in a few other precepts (#3, 7, 9, 10, 12, 18), the phrase *kokoro nashi* ("not heart/mind/thought") appears, ending the statement. This refrain emphasizes that this too is not something to disturb your heart/mind/thought with. In each case it is an injunction against keeping such elements of obfuscation from disturbing the clarity and balance of *kokoro* (*shin*: heart/mind).

Obviously, resentment and complaint, bearing a grudge or other such grievances against the way things are, reveal an expectation that things should be otherwise, according to our own desires or preferences. In a way, these are the worst form of attachment because they are about things that don't actually exist. Resentment and complaint are the worst forms of regret because they regret the actions of others over which one had no control to begin with.

Clearly these are not appropriate in or for oneself or others, but also not directed at oneself or others. Yet for those complainers among us, no amount of exhortation will stop their whining because they have become accustomed to their victimhood.

10 "Do not let yourself be guided by love."

This injunction suggests a coldness of heart, a detachment necessary for a warrior who cannot be swayed to go into or stay out of battle for sentimental reasons, but it can also be interpreted less harshly, more liberally for our bodhisattva practice. The suggestion is that love, especially romantic or lustful love, is dangerous for the clear mind/heart; that one's path should not be dictated by feelings alone. We have all perhaps made unwise decisions in our lives based on what we thought were the dictates of the heart. We are taught, in fact, in countless works of literature and popular culture that we should be guided by the heart, or rather by sentiment. Afraid of being accused of heartlessness, we sometimes accede to unwise actions or decisions that will actually in the end cause not only ourselves but also others more harm than good. But we feel we have no choice because of the dictates of a sentimentalist ideology that is akin to blind faith or love-it-or-leave-it patriotism.

Here it is important to note that *kokoro* (Japanese) or *shin* (Chinese) does not mean the same as our Western "heart." For us, it is natural to separate heart and mind, feelings from thought, and thus we often feel that we have to make a choice between heart and mind, between doing what feels right and what we think is right. In such cases we say we are "of two minds" on the matter, or that we are "conflicted" or "divided" within ourselves. We cannot come to the decision with a "whole heart," or what should really be called a "whole heart/mind."

How often a feeling comes disguised in thought's clothing. How often a thought comes disguised as feeling (inspiration). That clothing is often just a rationalization for a decision we have made with our gut (i.e., our heart), a way of propping up with irrelevant logic or evidence what may or may not be a bad decision based entirely on a feeling.

Better to act with one heart/mind (kokoro), to understand that they are really one thing with two faces, often looking in opposite directions, pulling us toward different paths, but really a whole thought if only we could look at it with a whole heart. The path we choose though should be only the Way, and to get to that path we need to unify heart/mind so that we don't mistake the wolf in a wool sweater for the sheep.

This edict is not so much about whether Musashi was homosexual, as some argue. Indeed there may be some sense of male warrior "homosocial" bonding, as there was for the Greek Spartans. It is not even whether romantic love is to be avoided. At least for us, as bodhisattva samurai, it means that we should act according to what is best for our loved ones and not what we feel will most evidently express our love for them in the short term or on the surface. We are retainers for our loved ones: we protect and defend, but sentiment must be one of the evils we protect them against, our own sentimentality one of the seductions we defend them against.

Do not let yourself be led by the nose, the sex organs, or the heart.

11 "In all things, do not have any preferences."

This is the heart of the matter. In this, the central tenet of the *Dokkodo*, sitting at the midpoint of the twenty-one exhortations to his disciple, Musashi echoes the opening lines of the *Shinjinmei*. Preferences are the first symptoms of desire. Preferences are the first symptoms of suffering. Preferences kill Zen practice. Preferences kill zazen.

We see this in the dojo almost every day. One person would rather sit in the morning, another at night. One person would rather the heat be turned up, another the air conditioning. One person would rather sit for thirty minutes, another for forty or fifty. One person would rather have a shorter ceremony or no ceremony at all, while another wants more ceremony. Once you begin to say, "I'd rather this than that," there is no end to 'druthers. And our 'druthers immediately put us into conflict with the 'druthers of others. This can sometimes work out nicely: I prefer the blue M&Ms

while you prefer red. But what if we both prefer blue? Love triangles are based on such conflicts, leading to unhappiness or even tragedy, and the result of a momentary preference is ten thousand years of drama.

You might recall David Chadwick's story about how one of Shunryu Suzuki's disciples thought they should sit for thirty minutes instead of forty because this would attract more practitioners, many of whom found forty minutes just too long. Suzuki pretended to consider the proposal, then said: "I have been thinking we should sit for fifty minutes. Hmmmm. I've got an idea! Let's compromise and sit for forty minutes."

This story is a classic anecdote about preferences and how everyone has them. It also illustrates the first tenet, though, that says "do not go against what has been established by tradition." At least one should not change lightly what is already established or simply to get some advantage, such as more practitioners.

I have been through numerous sangha meetings to discuss ways of increasing membership. The pattern of the discussion is always the same: 1) we would like to encourage more members to join and do zazen; 2) in addition to letting people know that our group exists, what changes in our practice might make us more welcoming? Then, either 3a) the changes are made and no significant or lasting increase is seen, or 3b) the changes are not made and no significant or lasting increase is seen. In either case, 4) we conclude that those who seek the practice will find it if it is accessible and those who are not really interested in the practice will not come under any circumstances. Changes to the practice sometimes make a small or short-term difference, but those who persevere do so whether the changes are made or not.

It doesn't matter what the changes are. Sometimes it is a change in the time of the sitting (late morning instead of early morning; Saturday instead of Sunday; Wednesday instead of Tuesday evening). Sometimes it is a matter of cost (five dollar sittings, one dollar sittings, free sittings). It doesn't matter. The ones devoted to the practice will be devoted to the practice under any reasonable conditions, and those not devoted to the practice will never be no matter what concessions are made to their preferences. Why? Because preferences are illusions, and concessions to illusion are bound to be ineffective and illusory.

Such popularizing moves are just proselytizing or self-indulgence. While it is always good to increase awareness, visibility, and access to zazen, to change the practice simply to attract more practitioners is to pander to the lowest common denominator and rarely has any beneficial lasting effects. We should be flexible, but we should not dilute the practice to suit a preference, whether that preference be easier sitting or a larger sangha. Zen practice is likely to remain in most communities a small percentage of people, and we should not forget that small sanghas have their advantages. Better a thousand dojos with a dozen practitioners each than a dozen dojos with a thousand practitioners each. Small sanghas tend to be less prone to the divisions that come from more resources, more egos, or a charismatic teacher who can abuse power—in short, more preferences.

When I first started attending the New Orleans Zen Temple, I thought I might have preferred a Rinzai teacher or a Soto teacher who was not Robert Livingston Roshi, one who was gentler, less critical, one who taught with more words and less work, and so on. I sat through those preferences. I even left for several years, only to realize that it was senseless to follow my own preferences since these had not been much help to me in my life thus far. Instead, I discovered that by following the practice without regard for my own preferences was indeed "my own way," after all, and much more authentically my own way than if I had followed my preferences. Frank Sinatra was wrong. Doing it "My Way" is almost always a matter of posturing and hot air. Better to follow *The* Way because attainment is always indirect.

The *Dokkodo* is called "The Way to Be Followed Alone." It might also be called "The Way to follow *as* your own." To follow such a path is to become both a follower and a leader: and is there any better definition of a Zen master than one who finds a balance between following tradition and leading creatively alone? This is what I have observed in my master: this balance between leader and follower is the core of his wisdom. It is self-evident that to follow, one must have no preferences; it is just as true, though, that to lead, one must equally have no preferences. This is the Tao, balanced, the Middle Path. This is the way of whole heart abandonment.

12 *"Do not have any particular desire regarding your private domicile."*

While this is a corollary to other injunctions against desire and preferences, it is particularly relevant for a warrior who may have to bivouac at any time. For the bodhisattva or monk, it applies to communal living situations in monasteries or during intensive practice periods such as sesshin. Directing one's concentration away from the creature comforts one is used to and toward a focus on practice instead is good advice. Having no preference in regard to one's shelter or food makes harmonizing with others much easier. Conflict almost always arises when one person in a communal situation singles himself or herself out by drawing attention to his or her desires, whether these are voiced or not. Whether it is a question of temperature, mattresses, bedclothes, room assignments, work assignments, or menus it is always best to make no fuss. Fussiness is not a characteristic of the samurai, even less of the bodhisattva.

Public spaces such as dojo or temple are another matter. One must take care of shared spaces as one would maintain weapons, but this does not mean indulging one's desires about the space. Two anecdotes come to mind. The first is again from David Chadwick's recollections of Suzuki, describing how someone had straightened a picture frame in the dojo, only to have Suzuki come in and, always vigilant, make it crooked again. The second is from my own experience, when one of my students could not stand the ticking of the wall clock. It was not particularly loud, but once you allow yourself to focus on anything, no matter how minor, it can be magnified to painful proportions. The ticking had become so painful that she had to have the clock removed from the room. She never realized that the ticking of the clock was not the offender; it was the ticking of her mind she could not stop. She could remove the clock from the room, but she could not remove time from her mind. If one should have no desires about one's private quarters, one should also have no preferences about the public spaces that are the private quarters of the sangha. We can extend Musashi's suggestion to include one's surroundings in general.

My master was always very particular about the conditions in the temple, even to the colors of the walls (the range of earth tones, from greens through yellows and browns to orange were acceptable; blues were forbidden). In the dojo, in particular, the temperature, the lighting, the arrangement of the altar, all had to be according to his specifications. He had been known (before my time) to use the rensaku on the person responsible for setting the thermostat improperly. If the lighting was too bright or too dark, he would adjust the dimmer switch on entering the dojo. If the greenery at each side of the Buddha and Kodo Sawaki statues on the altar was not properly fanned, he would rearrange it before offering incense. This attention to detail was not about his personal desires; it was about maintaining a space that was relatively immutable in a world of radical mutability. The dojo was the place of practice where the constant change of one's own mind was sufficient distraction from the business of paying attention to the great matter of posture and breathing.

Certainly the temple and dojo are places that deserve great attention to detail, not to satisfy one's particular desires but because a well-designed, uncluttered, and clean place is conducive to Zen practice. Keeping them in that condition is part of the practice. Our surroundings do not need to be uncomfortable or homely; they should be simple and aesthetically pleasing in a way that does not interfere with their function—a functional aesthetic that makes practice (concentration, focus, attentiveness, harmonizing) more efficient. On the other hand, like the warrior, the bodhisattva must be willing to give up both functionality and aesthetics at any time and move on when the occasion calls.

13 "Do not pursue the taste of good food."
Food and shelter are equally necessities but equally to be taken as they come. It is easy to imagine—as high comedy—a

samurai as food critic or interior designer, even without John Belushi. Such discriminations, the rhetorical weapons of those who specialize in food and design, used for splitting hairs, are not the tools of the warrior which are used for splitting skulls, or the tools of the bodhisattva which are used for splitting the skulls of illusions.

Yet some of the best food I have tasted has been prepared in the Zen temple during sesshin. Is this a contradiction? I don't think so. One should not pursue good food for its taste. Good food, however, is requisite to keeping the human organism, the warrior's primary weapon, in good shape, its edges sharp. For the monk, too, good food is essential for focus and concentration. For anyone who has not completed a sesshin, it is worth emphasizing that sitting for hours is strenuous business, a real caloric conflagration, and serious sitting works up a healthy appetite. Dogen's *Instructions to the Tenzo*, the classic treatise on the importance of the head cook in a monastic setting, shows why the tenzo is second only to the abbot in a monastery: his food is the wholesome fuel on which the monks run.

In our sangha, my master would often lavish more attention on what was going on in the kitchen than in the dojo. Robert never gave Dharma talks or teisho; he did not lecture. His kusen were very simple and direct, to the point. His greatest teaching moments were in the kitchen or garden during samu. Robert expected the food to be not only wholesome, made of the best ingredients, but also delicious. This was not an idle desire or preference. Meals were a time to demonstrate the earnestness of one's practice, a performance of one's concentration in the art of cooking, no less important than one's ability to sit with correct posture or to play the instruments in the ceremony. Taste is not always about "taste."

14 "Do not possess ancient objects intended to be preserved for the future."

Like food critics and interior designers, collectors of art and antiques have nothing in common with the warrior. Tendencies toward attachment and accumulation are weaknesses on the battlefield, and these tendencies can be seen in the impulse to acquisitiveness. The desire to acquire antiques or valuable objects as investments may seem prudent, or to protect them for posterity may seem noble, but these are actually mild forms of hoarding.

Musashi himself gave away all of his possessions before retreating to a cave at the age of sixty to write the *Gorin no sho* and the *Dokkodo*. Having reached this age myself recently, I understand his urge to disburden himself of things he may not need. Getting rid of excess cleared his mind for the concentration required to write the "Scroll of Heaven" (the scroll of ku or emptiness) that concludes the *Gorin no sho*:

> Know this state of mind and take as fundamental that which is straight, conceived of the way with a sincere mind, practice strategy broadly, think on a large scale with accuracy and clarity, think of *void* as the way and see the way as *void*.
>
> In emptiness the good exists and evil does not exist.
>
> Knowing exists, the principle exists, the way exists, and the mind—is void (*ku*).

How could a collection of knickknacks or valuable antiques increase the value of the void or bring us more readily to this realization?

Cousin to the hoarder is the collector. But also those who buy and sell art and antiques miss the opportunity to follow the Way. Making "a profession out of selling the arts," Musashi says in the *Gorin no sho*, applies as well to artists who "treat themselves as articles of merchandise and produce objects with a view to selling them. This attitude is tantamount to the act of separating the flower from the fruit." While this purity of intention in regard to the arts may be laudable, it is also a reflection of an aristocracy of spirit both uncompromising and unfeasible for all who do not subsist on the largesse of a patron or on personal riches or trust funds. Today, we are far more inclined to accept a different standard of "right livelihood," which would more readily accept selling one's art than practicing the art of killing, which was Musashi's livelihood. Yet there are many devoted Buddhists in the military whose livelihood is still just that: the art of war. They deserve a bow of gratitude, for the military should not be left to the barbarians.

15 *"Do not follow customary beliefs."*
This is perhaps the most radical of Musashi's twenty-one tenets. For Japanese society, tradition trumps originality, as we saw in the first tenet which seems to contradict this one. How do we reconcile "do not go against tradition" with "do not follow custom"? An undeniable tension divides these two demands. No amount of rationalization will reconcile them. Their mutual exclusion must be confronted experientially with one's whole being as one would embrace a koan.

Ideals are fine in the abstract, but they can get in the way of what needs to be done in the moment. This is why all ideas and ideals must be emptied out of the warrior's heart when it comes time to act. A general rule that one must not rush into battle may well need to be thrown out the window when a specific situation calls for a quick decision and quicker action. Customary beliefs may fit what has already happened or what usually happens but they may not fit the needs of the present moment. Thus it is as necessary to shed such beliefs as it is for an animal to shed fur in the summer, or a snake to shed its skin, or a monk to shed body and mind. Those customary beliefs, in fact, include all tradition, what has been taught by fathers, teachers, masters, even the Buddha himself because no "ism" can help you in the battlefield, no buddha can ease your sore knees on your zafu, no buddha that is but you.

16 *"Do not seek especially either to collect or to practice arms beyond what is useful."*

Here again, accumulation for its own sake is a form of attachment, an indulgence of preferences, a concession to the whims of the ego, even if what is being collected are skills. Practicing arms for their own sake Musashi also discouraged. He would probably scoff, for example, at reenactment enthusiasts who practice outdated methods of fence or warfare for their own sake. He was always interested in what was functional over what was just going to confer either status or pleasure. He was an artist, but when it came to the weapons of war he was not attached to the aesthetics of weapons. The weapons at hand were the ones to use, not the ones that would look good over the fireplace.

A warrior needs to have available the full range of abilities and weapons. One should not prefer one weapon over another. On the other hand, one should know what one's strengths are and adapt those to the situation, paying attention to one's aptitudes for one weapon over another. As he says in the *Gorin no sho*, "Weapons should be adapted to your personal qualities and be the ones you can handle. It is useless to imitate others. For a general as for a soldier, it is negative to have marked preferences." He puts a point on this, as he often does when there is potential for ambiguity or contradiction in what he has said, by concluding: "You should examine this point well."

For the bodhisattva, examining this point might include, instead of weapons, whatever the tools of his or her trade are. A gardener need not collect tools that are interesting historic relics of bygone modes of agriculture. A writer need not collect pens and typewriters and early computers but only the writing technology that is most useful for her in the present, using whatever is best suited to her abilities and her project's needs. Neither does an orchid grower need to also grow all his own vegetables, nor a writer to write sonnets as well as cookbooks. This may sound odd coming from someone who has published in many genres, but I speak from experience. Dispersing one's energies can be wasteful.

17 *"Do not shun death in the way."*
This is at once the clearest, most unambiguous of Musashi's statements. It would appear to be reserved entirely for samurai, for whom death is an occupational hazard, yet it should have the same urgency and relevance for contemporary bodhisattva practice. Musashi acknowledges

that others' ways are distinct from the way of the warrior, but he also recognizes that certain principles are common to all. Specific teachings can be interpreted or "polished" in each person's own way. For example, "a warrior must always have in his mind ... the way of death. But the way of death is not reserved only for warriors. A monk, a woman, a peasant—any person—can resolve to die for the sake of a social obligation or honor." Quaint fanaticism from a bygone era? Or a model of behavior for our corrupt and cowardly, self-serving age?

Hakuin said, "Young people! Do you fear death? Die now, then!" If we did not know better, or we did not know Hakuin, we might think he was encouraging young people to commit suicide, to just get it over with since life is not worth living if it is filled with fear. But we know that Hakuin is really saying that if you face your greatest fears here and now and often, then you will push past them and live a life devoid of fear. If you die to your current self, you can live the rest of your life in clarity and balance. And since we climb into our coffins during zazen, we can climb out again without fear.

It is not death itself that is the Great Matter that is spoken of in Zen. The Great Matter is how to live in the face of death. Only doubt about the Great Matter makes us tremble, but how can we live without doubt? How can we live without facing the Great Doubt? If we dispel Doubt (through faith or certainty or some other absolute) then we rob ourselves of the urgency of here and now. The real question is: how do we preserve Doubt and Certainty together? How do we embrace Death and Life at the same time, in the same breath? It is not a matter of choosing. It is a matter of what Arthur Braverman has called "living and dying in zazen."

18 "Do not seek to possess either goods or fiefs for your old age."

Another form of attachment and accumulation, saving up for one's old age is presumptuous. It assumes that one will live that long, for one thing. How can one who follows the Way both not shun death and put money away for retirement? This does not mean, however, that one should not take care of oneself, nor that one should not make preparations for unforeseen contingencies, only that material goods and power are not to be stored up. Generosity would demand that when we are flush with goods or fiefs we should be able to dispense with them easily, giving them away in a spirit of philanthropy. We should be able to drop these concerns rather than gather them together. Of course, Musashi did not live past sixty or sixty-one (his age when he wrote the *Dokkodo* and my age as I write), and it is surprising that he lived that long, considering the battles he was in and duels he fought. The idea, though, is that one does not become attached to material things or to power or stature and that these can be shuffled off as easily as this mortal coil.

19 "Respect Buddha and the gods without counting on their help."

Whether or not prayer as petition is useless, as Jim Morrison contends in the Doors song "The End," when he screams, "You *cannot* petition the Lord with prayer!", the idea of a personal deity, one that would "save" you in battle or in any other way is unimaginable to Musashi. We pay our respect not for what we might receive in return in a relationship with Buddha or the gods but from a sense of our relative inconsequence in the universe, that we are all subject to the same conditions of dependent origination, and this includes the Buddha and the gods, as well as dogs and rocks. All existences deserve our respect, not just the Buddha and the gods. When we bow in the dojo, remember, we do not bow to a statue of the Buddha, much less to the Buddha himself; we bow in a gesture of respect for all existences and to their Buddha nature, which is empty.

What is Buddha nature? It is the nature that we share in respect to what the Buddha taught in terms of dependent origination, insubstantial identity (no self), and ku (emptiness). We are all in this mortal form for just a while, and these elements that do not take mortal (or sentient) form now, will or could be very like us someday. Thus we bow to all existences, even those that are made up, like the gods, just as we would to other art forms, like the characters of fiction, or the images of poetry. We are that insubstantial. To rely on characters in fiction, to petition the images in poetry with prayer, and to expect some response in any crucial situation such as battle would be folly. So it is in all matters of life and death: our respect for the Buddha, the gods, and all existences must not atrophy into a reliance on them for assistance.

20 "You can abandon your own body, but you must hold on to your honor."

The Chinese expatriate Ma Jian now living in Paris has written a brilliant short story first published in *The New Yorker* in 2004 called "The Abandoner." Set in China in the early 1980s at the beginning of the one-child policy era, the story concerns a minor local government official known as the vice-chairman, and his "retarded" daughter. He and his wife want a son, so they apply for and receive a waiver, but alas the second child is also a daughter. He decides to take the retarded daughter, Miaomiao, to another village and abandon her, so he and his wife can replace her with the boy they always wanted. Over the course of several years he takes Miaomiao to orphanages or neighboring villages, and each time he finds an excuse not to go through with the abandonment. He leaves cash on her for her support, but people come and steal it or try to take her clothes. He chases after them, retrieves the cash, and takes her home again.

As episodes like this accrue, we see a change in him. The experience of "abandoning" her becomes their bond, a ritual outing the way other fathers might take their daughters to the playground or the zoo, and "each time he tried to get rid of Miaomiao he felt his attachment to her deepen . . . His trips with Miaomiao had made him appreciate his life, and, in a way, he was grateful to her." Finally, in coming to terms with the way things are instead of going against what he calls his "fate" he comes to realize that he will be happier if he simply does what needs to be done. "Each time he tried to abandon Miaomiao, he felt as though he were, in fact, abandoning himself, and the future that had been fated for him." Indeed, this is the point of the story, indicated by the fact that in Chinese the title can mean either "the abandoner" or "the abandoned." They are interchangeable, just as, in a sense, when he refers to Miaomiao as "retarded," we sense that it is really he who is retarded (from the Latin: *retardare*, "delayed, hindered, kept back") in his spiritual realization by his own war against his fate.

The vice-chairman is not only trying to abandon his own body (his daughter, his karma, his fate), but he is more importantly abandoning his honor. He seems to hear Miaomiao speak to him:

> Over the past two years, I have had to assume the role of the abandoned child. I have gained my own identity, and through your struggles with me you have learned some lessons about life. A father can fool a retarded child, but a retarded child can also fool her father. I have given a pattern to your life, a rhythm. I have taught you things about yourself you would have preferred not to know. You must understand that your mission will destroy you in the end. In a deranged world, only the retarded can find happiness . . . I am not even sure that I exist. If you were retarded like me, you would understand what I am saying. I wish you would give up this futile mission of yours. You've done your best for everyone. You have let neither me nor yourself down. There's nothing more you can do.
> *http://www.newyorker.com/magazine/2004/05/10/ the-abandoner*

The story ends with this becoming the pattern of their life together, a continual abandonment that is not really abandonment but rather the vehicle of a strong and growing attachment that gives meaning to his life. He transcends his cultural and metaphysical fate and even his own narrative of desire by coming to accept and thereby benefit from reality. Another way of saying this is: "Delusion itself is satori." He is no longer fixated on what he would like to happen because it is always our cultural, societal, or personal desires that create suffering and retard awakening. His enlightenment to his true nature is to see that his original face, if you will, is that of the "retarded" Miaomiao, no different, utterly interrelated with other existences, especially those with whom we are most in contact, and those for whom we are karmically responsible. In attempting to abandon Miaomiao he was attempting to abandon not only himself but also the very means of his awakening to what is most important in reality. Although his new dedication to his "fate" is not consciously avowed, we can see that he has regained his honor by abandoning his resolve to abandon her. In failing to abandon her, he also fails to abandon his honor.

In contrast to the dishonorable way the vice-chairman behaves toward his daughter in attempting to disown her are stories of monks who took on the responsibilities of raising children not their own. Hakuin (or in some cases it is told of Hunan) was supposed to have been accused of being the father of young girl's child. Instead of denying the accusation, he took the child and raised it as his own until the mother recanted and took the child back. He faced the accusation and the recantation with equal equanimity, neither refusing the child a home with him nor clinging to the child when it was taken away. Similarly, Tokujoo (Kozan Kato), the good friend of Kodo Sawaki whose story is recounted in Arthur Braverman's novel based on their friendship, *Dharma Brothers*, took in a novice who had become pregnant and found the fulfillment of his life in living with her and raising this child as his own. This becomes Tokujoo's life koan, but his teacher gives him another that prepares him to deal with the real situation. The koan his teacher gives him concerns an old woman who burns down a monk's hut because he turns down the advances of a young woman. Ultimately, he realizes that his own path is not as some ideal celibate monk but the more difficult path of householder-monk. In each case, Hakuin's and Tokujoo's, abandonment occurs on two levels: an abandonment that is a karmic action and an abandonment that cuts the karmic action. In the first case, a young woman is abandoned and she in turn abandons her child to a monk; the monk, in a compassionate act that reverses the karma of the first abandonment, abandons his own preferences to take on the responsibility of raising the child. In the second case, a young woman is again abandoned; another monk, in a similar act of compassion that also provides his own awakening, abandons his plans of renouncing (abandoning) the world and instead takes on additional worldly responsibilities, which allows him to discover his true purpose in life. Again, "delusion itself is satori."

I feel a personal affinity to this word, abandonment. As part of the ordination ceremony, the master confers a Dharma name on the new bodhisattva or monk. As Robert looked me in the eyes and handed over my kesa through the billowing cloud of incense, he called me by my monastic name: "Taisen, or Great Abandonment."

Dharma names come in many forms. They can be inspired by the person's character or potential, or by the sounds of their given names. Some masters allow students to choose or suggest their own names. Dharma names can be descriptive or predictive, emphasizing an existing quality as a caricature, or encouraging one's potential as a prophecy or positive thinking. In any case, they have about them an aura of destiny. Of course my immediate reaction was that Taisen was the bodhisattva name of Deshimaru and that I was completely unworthy of it, that it was a name that, like a great ballplayer's jersey number, should be retired. After that first reaction, I am still discovering, like the vast countryside of a koan, the dimensions implied by "Great Abandonment."

The strength of my practice, such as it is, has come about through "great abandonments" in my life. On the day I walked into the New Orleans Zen Temple—January 27, 2001 (which also happened to be my master's birthday)—I felt a sense of destiny. It was as though I had shrugged off my previous life and left it outside the door. Over the course of my sixty-plus years, I have left many selves behind, living a succession of lives. This transformation, however, was all the more radical for being almost unnoticeable from the outside. Inside, however, it was a complete metamorphosis. Work and family continued as before, except now with increased significance. Suddenly, I was not the most important thing in my life. I became more successful at work through increased abilities of concentration and attention, and my career took a steady course. My health improved with my posture. My ability to confront even the most devastating personal losses and psychological affronts, not to mention natural and economic disasters, surprised even me. I did not abandon the things of the world but instead learned to care for them even more, finding balance in an unbalanced world, and satori in delusion itself.

I had abandoned myself to the way of the bodhisattva. As my practice intensified over the next five years, my duties at the temple increased, becoming Robert's assistant, editing and publishing books for the sangha, and Robert put me in charge of training. Later, as I took monastic ordination and assumed the duties of a teacher, the responsibilities to Zen practice increased. Paradoxically, instead of taking time away from my devotion to work and family, my devotion to them increased in parallel intensity. Abandonment did not mean leaving anything behind. There is no such thing as parallel lives, only this one life lived fully.

I suspect there will be more abandonments in the future. Because one has trained and matured in the practice gradually, it makes it easier to follow the path spontaneously, naturally, automatically. When transitions occur, when mujo strikes, it makes it easier not to stray from the Way.

21 "Never stray from the way of strategy."

Discipline and determination: these are the hallmarks of Zen practice. They are not unique to Zen practice, but without them there is no Zen practice. With them, all else is possible. Bodhidharma, who was also the founder of martial arts, is the icon of this path. Avalokiteshvara and Buddha represent compassionate wisdom and serenity, but Bodhidharma is the furrowed brow of discipline and determination in the practice that brings compassion and serenity. While the Buddha is best represented in *paranirvana*, having achieved his goal at the end of this life, Bodhidharma sitting in zazen is the model for bodhisattva practice in this life, without goal (mushotoku).

Self-styled "Buddhists" so often have a goal: they want to attain directly what they imagine the Buddha had—serenity or compassion or unflappable wisdom. The Nichiren sect can "pray" for their desires, and Theravadans can go after nirvana as *arhats* in this life, while those with a literal belief in reincarnation might place their bets on better-luck-next-time. In Zen practice we rely on here and now; we reject goals; we persevere and "polish" our practice, not to make a mirror out of a tile but to polish a tile. We practice for the sake of practice, which is another way of saying we practice for the sake of all existences. Everything else is so much window-dressing, fluff, wishful-thinking, and pious posturing.

"Not easy, not difficult," my master always says, "but you must make an effort." Bodhidharma shows us the way of that effort: not easy, not difficult. Musashi echoes that teaching, affirming that the Way itself is the effort, effort itself is the Way. This is what it means not to stray: it means that we never stop putting forth the effort, for heroism is not in victory or defeat but only in right effort regardless of the outcome. This is how we achieve balance in an unbalanced world. It is how we discover balance in ourselves. Of the twenty-one theses of Musashi, this is truly the only dictum we need; like zazen, it contains all the others. Not straying from the Way—whether it is the way of strategy or the way or zazen—is essential. Just as the *Shinjinmei* can be summed up in its opening lines, "Just don't discriminate, just don't choose, just have no preferences," and just as zazen contains all the bodhisattva precepts, so this—"Never stray from the Way"—contains all the other "thou shalt nots," prohibitions, and injunctions of the *Dokkodo*. Just do zazen; just follow the Way. "How long must we practice zazen?" students used to ask Deshimaru. The answer is clear: "Until you die."

GLOSSARY

The definitions here are not meant to cover every usage of the terms. Since practices at centers, temples, and monasteries vary widely, these terms can mean very different things depending on the current interpretation of any one lineage's tradition. These definitions are intended to convey the sense of these terms as practiced primarily in the American lineage of Taisen Deshimaru through Robert Livingston Roshi and the New Orleans Zen Temple and its affiliates in Louisiana, Mississippi, and California. However, there will be similarities in Deshimaru lineage dojos throughout the world, from Australia and Africa to Europe and South America.

A note on pronunciation: Japanese words tend to be phonetic and unaccented, with each syllable sharing the emphasis equally.

arhat: an enlightened person, a sage, or immortal.

Avalokiteshvara: bodhisattva of compassionate wisdom. Guanyin (Chinese) or Kannon (Japanese).

Bodhidharma: fifth or sixth-century monk who brought Zen to China from India. Supposed to have created martial arts at the Shaolin monastery where he practiced for nine years. Ta Mo (Chinese) or Daruma (Japanese).

bodhisattva: one who practices the way to help others. Bodhisattva (lay) ordination consists of a ceremony in which the teacher gives the student a rakusu (or small kesa, most often sewn by the student or a member of the extended sangha) inscribed with his or her Dharma (Buddhist) name. Taking bodhisattva ordination is primarily an expression of one's devotion to the practice of zazen.

bonno: "troublesome-suffering." Often translated as "sin," bonno can also be read as "delusion," "illusion," or "attachment," which also fit the description of sins. I prefer to think of bonno in less religiously accented language, though, as what we might call "issues," as in "I've been unable to get over my issues." We once had a Japanese resident at the temple in New Orleans who had come to get away from his bonno back home, by which he meant a whole variety of concerns, from parental and societal expectations to his own bad habits.

bonno soku bodai: "Delusion itself is satori." Or, as it says in the *Shodoka*, "The true nature of delusion is Buddha-nature."

budo: the way of martial arts.

Deshimaru, Taisen (1914-1982): Japanese Soto Zen Master, based in Paris, who brought Zen to Europe and the West.

Dogen, Eihei (1200-1253): Japanese Zen Master who brought Soto Zen to Japan from China.

Dharma: cosmic truth, or the adequate representation of that truth in the teachings of the Way.

dukkha: suffering. Basis of the first noble truth of the Buddha, that life is never exactly what we want it to be, always unsatisfactory, thus we suffer.

dojo: the place where we practice the Way (*do*) through zazen, kinhin, and ceremony. Sometimes used interchangeably with zendo.

dokusan: private interview with the teacher or master. While a formal etiquette is established for entering and leaving the dokusan room, the interview itself can be as informal as necessary. Dokusan can be requested by either teacher or student, in or out of sesshin. Somewhat rare in comparison to Rinzai practice, where koans are regularly tested in dokusan.

Fukanzazengi: "Universal Recommendation for Zazen." Basic zazen instruction by Dogen, sometimes chanted.

fuse: a gift given without thought of return from a practitioner to a temple or master in the form of material or monetary goods. Teaching is the master's fuse to the student, considered the highest fuse.

gassho: putting the hands together in front of the face, usually accompanied by a bow. A gesture of respect for all existences. The word is often used as a closing valediction in a letter in place of "yours truly" or "sincerely."

godo: the leader during zazen or ceremony.

genmai: "dark rice." In the Deshimaru lineage, traditional brown rice and vegetable soup eaten at breakfast.

gyoji: daily repetition of the practice, which might include zazen, ceremony, samu, or other activities.

han: the block of wood hanging outside the dojo, struck to announce the beginning and end of zazen. It often has an inscription that reads: "Life and death is a serious matter" or "Don't waste time."

Hannya Shingyo: the *Heart Sutra*, chanted after morning and sometimes evening zazen.

hara: the body's center in Zen practice. The region a few inches below the navel, deep in the abdomen, where ki, or energy, is generated and stored. The focus of concentration during zazen.

hishiryo: thinking not-thinking. The samadhi of zazen, absolute thought, beyond thinking and non-thinking.

inkin: a small bell mounted on a handle and rung with a metal striker to accompany the godo's movements.

jiriki: self power, coming from one's own discipline and practice. The power of Zen.

kai: precepts or vows.

karma: action and its causes and effects.

Keizan, Jokin (1267-1365): Great Japanese Soto Zen Master, author of *Denkoroku: Record of the Transmission of the Light* (circa 1300).

kesa: the robe of the transmission, sewn by hand and received upon monastic ordination. Worn over the left shoulder.

kinhin: walking zazen.

koan: the "cases," or stories that pose a problem to be worked out by a student in the course of practice. These cases cannot be solved intellectually but can only be embraced with the entire being. In Rinzai Zen, koan study forms a kind of curriculum. In Soto Zen, koans provide a literary culture. The best koans come from one's own experience.

kontin: "darkness-sinking." The mind sinking into drowsiness or depression.

ku: emptiness.

kusen: spontaneous oral teaching given during zazen.

kyosaku: "wake-up stick." A hardwood stick usually of oak, poplar, or ash, between two and three feet in length and flat at one end. It is requested by the person sitting in zazen by holding their hands in gassho. A blow to acupressure points on each shoulder can be instantly tonic and restorative. Also, the person who wields the kyosaku.

kyosakuman: person administering the kyosaku during zazen, usually a senior member of the sangha. Also called junko or simply kyosaku.

Mahayana: "The Great Vehicle" branch of Buddhism, which includes Zen and Tibetan strains. Implies the bodhisattva ideal of practice for the sake of others.

Manjusri: bodhisattva of wisdom, carries a sword to cut delusion. Monju (Japanese).

mokugyo: hollow wooden drum used to keep time during chanting the *Hannya Shingyo*.

mondo: teaching in the form of a question-and-answer dialog between master and disciples. Many koans have their origin in a mondo, real or fictional.

mu: "no, not." Famous koan, often the first and most difficult koan students study. Does a dog have Buddha nature? Mu!

mudra: a hand gesture. In Buddhist iconography there are dozens of gestures with symbolic meanings, including the hand held up palm outward, the mudra of "no fear."

muga: no self, no ego. *Anatta, anatman.*

Muhozan Kozenji: "Peakless Mountain, Shoreless River Temple," the New Orleans Zen Temple.

mujo: impermanence, mutability, constant change.

Musashi, Miyamoto (c. 1584-1645): also known by his Buddhist name Niten Doraku. Legendary swordsman and ronin, disciple of the Zen monk Takuan, and author of *The Way of Five Rings* and the *Dokkodo.*

mushotoku: attitude of no profit, no goal, no personal gain, essential to genuine Zen practice.

nirvana: extinguishment, freed of the round of samsara, death.

paranirvana: nirvana after death; the posture of Shakyamuni Buddha on his deathbed.

raihai: bowing and prostrations. According to Deshimaru, an essential part of Zen practice, the complement to zazen.

rakusu: small, symbolic five-band kesa given from the teacher to the student during bodhisattva and monastic ordination and other special occasions.

rensaku: use of the kyosaku as a form of "education" or punishment.

roshi: Zen master. An honorific form of address for any master who has received the shiho but usually reserved for an elderly master.

sampai: three pai, or prostrations. Like gassho, a gesture of respect for all existences.

samsara: cycle of life and rebirth, the illusory phenomena of the world.

samu: work practice. Can take a variety of forms, including sewing the rakusu or kesa (especially for someone else), office work for the sangha, or more commonly any physical labor.

sangha: group of practitioners. This community can be interpreted as narrowly as those in the room, those associated with the temple or center, the entire lineage past and present, or most broadly all existences.

sanran: "dispersed-confused." Scattered overactivity of the mind.

satori: awakening.

Sawaki, Kodo (1880-1965): reformer who reinvigorated Japanese Zen by emphasizing the practice of zazen over ceremony and scholarship. Often called "Homeless Kodo" because he had no fixed temple until he settled at Antaiji, where he died.

seiza: kneeling posture, with or without a zafu or low bench.

sesshin: "to touch the mind." A Zen retreat from one to several days or weeks.

Shariputra: cleverest disciple of Buddha, interlocutor of the *Heart Sutra*.

shikantaza: "only just sitting." Zazen practice of concentration without object or goal.

shiki: phenomena, form.

shin jin datsu raku: "mind and body drop off."

shinjinmei: trust or faith in heart-mind.

shippei: bamboo staff used in the shusso ceremony as a symbol of the transfer of authority from master to disciple. Referred to in the ceremony as the "three-foot long black snake."

shusso: chief assistant to the master, or head monk in charge of training. In the shusso ceremony, during sesshin, a monk is given authorization to teach.

Soto: one of the chief schools of Zen Buddhism.

sunyata: ku, emptiness.

sutra: any important text in Buddhism considered to be directly from the Buddha or on the same level as one from the Buddha.

tathata: suchness. The miracle of everyday reality, such as it is.

tariki: other power, as in the power of faith in a power outside oneself. The power of Pure Land Buddhism.

teisho: oral teaching, Dharma talk or lecture, given outside of zazen.

tenzo: temple or sesshin cook.

umpan: metal in the shape of a cloud. Basically a dinner bell, played at the end of morning zazen before genmai and before each meal during sesshin.

Vimalakirti: enlightened lay person of Mahayana practice, contemporary of Buddha, subject of the *Vimalakirti Nirdesa Sutra*.

zafu: round cushion, usually stuffed with kapok, used for zazen.

zagu: rectangular cloth laid out by a monk for sitting and bowing.

zazen: sitting concentration.

zendo: alternate but not preferred term for dojo. Short for "zazendo."

Zenji: a title given to the head of Eiheiji or Sojiji, the two chief training temples in Japanese Soto Zen Buddhism. Also conferred posthumously as an honorific to prominent or legendary masters, such as Dogen and Keizan.

INDEX

9/11: 7

"The Abandoner" (Jian): 235-38
Abandonment: 5, 36, 165, 172, 225, **235-241**
Absorption (*see also* Concentration): **143-144**, 148-49
Adam and Eve: 168
Alcohol: 100-01, 166, 191
Ambition: 10, 91, 215
Anatta (see also *Muga*): 23; implied, 98
Anatman (see also *Anatta, Muga*): 23
Artists: 105-06, 230-31
Art: 28, 70-71, 75, 90, 99, 229-30, 235; of cooking: 228; of sitting and forgetting: 38, 62, 155; of the warrior: 199; martial arts: 38, 61, 76, 105, 131, 200, 241
Attachment: **90-92**, 165, 212-20, 229, 231, 234-37
Attainment: 104, 210-11, 225, 241
Attitude of mind (*see also* Concentration): 4, **43-44, 68-69**; implied, 70-71; **81-82**
Auden, W. H.: 99
Austin, James H.: 134
Avalokiteshvara (bodhisattva): 241
Awakening: 27, 40, 140, 180, 237-39
Awareness: 28, 67, 76, **100-01**, 104, 110, 111, 148, 187-88, 215

Bakersfield Area Skeptics Society: xiii
Balance: xi, **75-76, 107-111**, 242
Beethoven, Ludwig van: 91-92
"Being-Time" (Dogen): 37
Being-Time (or Time-Being): 117-19
Beliefs: xiii, 22, 24-25, 29, 35-6, 41, 123-25, 153-54, 178, 181, 241; cultural beliefs: *karma*, 24-25, 41, 88, 167-70, 215; reincarnation, 24, 41, 124, 169-70;

Beliefs (*continued*)
vegetarianism, 24-25, 125; customary beliefs, 204, 230-231
Benefits of practice: 26, 44, 49, 52, 83, 101
Bergson, Henri: 118
Blake, William: 185, 191, 207
Blue Cliff Record (*see also* Koans): 157
Bodhi Tree: 168
Bodhidharma (Daruma, Ta Mo): xiv, 9, 94-95, 105-107, 241-42
Bodhisattva (*see also*: Avalokiteshvara, Hachiman, Jizo, Manjusri): 22, 54-55, 87, 165, **197-98, 209-11**, 225-28, 232, 240-42; Vows: 18, 50, 101-102, 149, 163, 166, 171, 175;
Body-mind (Mind-body): 48, 61-62, 65, 73-74, 75, 77, 81, 131, 143, 166, 189, 198
Bonno (*see also* Suffering): 1, 168, 171
Boredom: 59-60
Bow/ing: 10, 37, 138, **152**, 165, **170-171**, 235
Braverman, Arthur: 233, 238
Breathing: **43-44**, 48-49, 64, **66-69**, 73, 103
Buddha/s (*see also* Three Treasures): xiv, 78-79, 81-82, 106, 149, 152, 231; Buddha-nature: 1, 27, 185, 235; Finger Sarira: xi; Way: 50, 171
Buddhism/Buddhist: 21-4, 26-28, 35, 40-42, **124-25**, 154-55, 180, 217; American: 21, 200; to China: 63; in military: 230; Nichiren: 241; Theravada: 241; self-styled: 241
Buddhist Lay Ordination Lectures (Katagiri): 78
Budo: xiv, 198, 210
Bushido: 106

248

ABOUT THE AUTHOR

Richard Collins is a Zen teacher in the lineage of Taisen Deshimaru and Dean of Arts and Humanities at California State University, Bakersfield. He has held several research fellowships, including a Fulbright-Hays grant and a Fulbright Senior Lectureship. Collins has taught at the American University in Bulgaria, Louisiana State University, and Xavier University, where he was editor of the Xavier Review. He received monastic ordination from Robert Livingston Roshi, and helps to lead the New Orleans Zen Temple. He founded the Zen Fellowship of Alexandria (Louisiana) and the Zen Fellowship of Bakersfield.

Contact Information: American Zen Association: *info@nozt. org* and *www.nozt.org*; Richard Collins, Zen Fellowship of Bakersfield: taisenreishin@gmail.com

ABOUT HOHM PRESS

HOHM PRESS is committed to publishing books that provide readers with alternatives to the materialistic values of the current culture, and promote self-awareness, the recognition of interdependence, and compassion. Our subject areas include parenting, transpersonal psychology, religious studies, women's studies, the arts and poetry.

Contact Information: Hohm Press, .PO Box 4410, Chino Valley, Arizona, 86323; USA; 800-381-2700, or 928-636-3331; email: *hppublisher@cableone.net*

Visit our website at *www.hohmpress.com*